FEAR WINDOWS NO MORE

Gieg

Danny Goodman

Fear Windows No More

Danny Goodman

New York   London   Toronto   Sydney   Tokyo   Singapore

Brady Publishing

A Division of Prentice Hall Computer Publishing
15 Columbus Circle
New York, NY 10023

ISBN: 1-56686-081-4
Library of Congress Catalog No.: 93-8322

Printing Code: The rightmost double-digit number is the year of the book's printing; the rightmost single-digit number is the number of the book's printing. For example, 93-1 shows that the first printing of the book occurred in 1993.

96   95   94   93   4   3   2   1

Manufactured in the United States of America

About the Author

Danny Goodman has been translating high-tech information for non-technical readers since the mid 1970s. He is a frequent contributor to *Playboy*, in-flight magazines, and city magazines across the country. His personal computer writing history spans the time of early *PC Magazine* to *PC World*, *MacWorld*, and *MacUser*. An author of 14 books on personal computers, his *Complete HyperCard Handbook* was a bestseller and taught hundreds of thousands of newcomers worldwide how to program. With world-class information designer, Richard Saul Wurman, the *Danny Goodman's Macintosh Handbook* broke new ground in computer book organization and presentation. Danny lives in a small coastal community near San Francisco.

Acknowledgments

A number of people deserve recognition for their help in turning an idea into reality. Because their roles are equally important within their specialties, I thank these folks in alphabetical order: Kelly Dobbs, John Gieg, Bill Gladstone, Jono Hardjowirogo, Steve Ruddock, Sonya Schaefer, Nathan Shedroff, and Mike Violano. The biggest thanks goes to the perhaps thousands of people I've met over the years who rolled their eyes when they heard I worked with computers and then rattled on about how they need to figure out how to use a machine one of these days. Today is the day.

Credits

Publisher
Michael Violano

Acquisitions Director
Jono Hardjowirogo

Managing Editor
Kelly D. Dobbs

Editorial Assistant
Lisa Rose

Illustrator
John Leonard Gieg

Book Designers
Michele Laseau
Kevin Spear

Cover Designer
Jay Corpus

Indexer
C. Alan Small

Production Team
Diana Bigham, Katy Bodenmiller, Scott Cook, Tim Cox, Mark Enochs,
Linda Koopman, Tom Loveman, Beth Rago, Carrie Roth, Joe Ramon

Marketing Director
Lonny Stein

Marketing Coordinator
Laura Cadorette

Contents

Introduction

Why You're Afraid
(and What We're Going To Do About It)

Here is a scene familiar to many...Your airliner has just arrived in a city you've never visited before. You walk through the jetway into the strange airport terminal gate area. You have a job to do: visiting clients, some of whom you already know from telephone conversations; others are complete strangers. Appointments were set before you left home, and you obviously want to be prompt (even if one of the big shots you're seeing should keep you waiting in the lobby for an hour).

First, you have to find the rental car desks. Because you're not really sure where they are at this airport, you follow the signs to baggage claim and ground transportation.

"Do you want a subcompact, compact, midsize, standard, or luxury car?" the rental agent asks. You have a vague notion of what a luxury model might be (and the consequences of listing one on your expense report), but the others are up for grabs. "A midsize," you say after some hesitation, but with a forcefulness that implies you were really thinking about the differences among the models you would get at each size. After a few clicks on the agent's computer terminal comes the offer, "We can give you a Celestial, a 3000K, or a Palomino convertible." You've seen glimpses of TV ads for some of these as you flipped channels, but you don't have a clue which is the best car. "I'll take the Celestial," you say, shrugging your shoulders. A couple of minutes and a few "initial heres" later, the agent whips out the following verbal instructions for the umpteenth time today, "Take the escalator to the departure level, cross to the outer island, go to the blue zone, and flag down our green and red van. Next in line?" You turn away hoping to look like an old pro, but into your mind flood questions like, "Is that up or down? How much traffic do I have to cross to get to that outer island? How far is it, anyway? What were those colors again?"

Fortunately, you stumble your way to the island and wave down the van. Assuming that you survive the Tilt-a-Whirl ride to the rental lot, you get into a strange car whose dashboard is loaded with more buttons than you've ever seen. You're freezing, and the air conditioner is blowing full force—how do you turn this thing off? How do you find a radio station with the music or talk you like when you can't even figure out how to tune the stations? If it rains later, it will take several minutes to find the wiper control. If you go out to dinner with a client and reach the parking lot in the dark, you'll be fumbling for a headlight switch whose location and feel are not in your fingers. And when you later pull up to refill the gas on your way back, you'll wonder if the gas cap is on the left or right rear fender.

Hand scribbled in your date book are directions to your first stop. You check your watch and see that you're running late if the "it's about 20 minutes from the airport" advice was correct...and the highway isn't clogged. As you motor your way down unfamiliar roads, the only thing you know about where you are is that at the moment you're taking Fernwiler Boulevard until you reach the fourth stoplight. Your heart rate is certainly heading skyward as you can't find the industrial park driveway that "you can't miss." When you do pull in after your u-turn, all visitor parking spaces are taken, and every other spot you see has somebody's name painted on it. So you look for any spot in outer Mongolia.

After the hike in from the parking lot, you're almost hyperventilating when you announce yourself to the receptionist. You haven't met this client before, so you won't even know the face when the person comes through the door, bidding you to enter. How will your first impression be? Is your hair neat? Are your clothing apertures closed? Finally, you meet, enter the conference room, and exchange pleasantries. Then you start talking about the subject of your visit. Now you can relax, because you're in familiar territory, and you can do your job.

Fear Is Natural

A traveling executive may be loathe to admit it, but fear plays a big role in responses to things that happen along a trip. These fears arise from three sources:

1. Fear of the unknown, especially when technology is involved. ("How do I reach my appointment in time and turn on the wipers now that it's raining?")

2. Mystifying and overabundant terminology. ("Quick, do you want a subcompact, compact, standard, or midsize?")

3. Fear of looking foolish by asking questions to which you're convinced everyone else in the world has the answers. ("I hope signs tell me which escalator takes me to the departure level and where the—what color was that?—zone is.")

Doing the Job—with a Computer

When it comes to using a new personal computer for the first time, we all go through the same trepidation as the harried business traveler. We have a job to do, and the personal computer is one of the tools we can use to accomplish that job—and do the job better than without the machine, we hope. The same fears apply, however:

1. Fear of the unknown, especially when technology is involved. ("I never even figured out what all the knobs and levers did on my old typewriter, and now all these keyboard keys and cables are coming to get me!")

2. Mystifying and overabundant terminology. ("I don't understand half the advertisements for the computer I just bought.")

3. Fear of looking foolish by asking questions to which you're convinced everyone else in the world has the answers. ("I can't look stupid next to my neighbor's teenager.")

Step One: Relax

To overcome these justifiable fears, it's important to know that there isn't a person alive who knows absolutely everything about the personal computer on your desk, Windows, and all the software you may run (although you'll find lots of people who *think* they do). Even if you find a very knowledgeable PC guru, you know something far more valuable to you than all the technical wizardry: what you need to do for your job. That's why you have the job you do or have chosen a particular profession.

This distinction is important. To computer gurus, the computers are the end, the goal, the miracle without which the world implodes. To you, however, the computer is just another tool that can help you do the job. Incorporating the tool into your work comfortably means knowing basic skills so that you can focus on your work, without letting the computer get in your way. Ideally, operating the computer should feel as automatic as operating a vehicle to get from point A to point B; your focus is on point B and what you'll be doing when you get there, not on how internal combustion engines or bicycle gears work.

What We'll Do

My goal is to guide you through the unknown territory that is Microsoft Windows, making you work with the computer in the process. You cannot learn how to use anything without actually using it. For example, if you give those written directions to a new client's office to a taxi driver, how many trips will it take before you know how to get there yourself? But if you drive there yourself, by the third time, you probably won't even think about where you need to turn; you just do it.

I recognize that you are not setting out to be a computer expert. It's more important that you become comfortable enough with Windows operation to let you get on with your work life. Because you will inevitably run into things that you don't know or understand, I'll be showing you how to solve problems on your own, ask the right questions when necessary, and get answers quickly. If I can show you what to do when you don't know what to do, you will become an intelligent Macintosh user. In other words, you will *Fear Windows No More.*

How I Do It

My methods are simple. I've distilled the essence of using Windows productively into a series of short encounters, each of which builds on experience gained from previous encounters.

The first 16 encounters are mandatory; the remaining are optional in case earlier discussions have peaked your curiosity (or you suspect you may be having fun). In each encounter, I introduce essential Windows terminology and basic principles. I also provide a section in which you practice the principles on your PC so that you can get to feel the rhythms of working with Windows on your way to making things automatic. I even include some final questions to reinforce the subject, intended to expel your Windows fears—I call them exorcises.

Near the end of the book, you'll be ready to start putting Windows to work in your own environment (a recording of the theme song to *Born Free* would be suitable background music while reading).

Assumptions

Before you begin, be aware of the only assumptions I make about you and your PC: the PC is out of its box; the hardware is set up; and Windows is installed. The PC must be equipped with a mouse, because human minds are not well served by memorizing dozens of keyboard incantations. If you've purchased a PC yourself, follow the "Getting Started" instructions that came with the machine to make sure that the keyboard, mouse, and (if you need one) external monitor are connected. If you are coming to an existing PC in an office, the machine is probably already set up by its previous owner or the nearest PC guru. Don't worry when some screen displays in this book don't look exactly like yours: your machine will have a different collection of items than mine. The book, however, covers those items we all have in common.

We'll be working with Version 3.1 of Windows. If you have an earlier version, it's a good idea to purchase the upgrade from your software supplier.

Now, let's cut the malarkey and get on with it. After all, you have a job to do, and all this computer stuff is taking up valuable time.

The Keyboard

Goal

Gain familiarity with the PC keyboard, especially getting the feel of frequently used two-key combinations.

What You Will Need

Place the keyboard (or opened notebook computer) in front of you with the computer turned off.

Terms of Enfearment

numeric keypad	Control key
function keys	Alt key
arrow keys	Escape key
Enter key	

Briefing

Keyboard Layout(s)

Virtually every PC comes with the IBM-compatible standard 101-key keyboard or the Extended keyboard (see fig. 1.1). Therefore, all computers capable of running Microsoft Windows have—in one form or another—the same array of keyboard functions.

Figure 1.1

Standard 101-key keyboard and Extended keyboard layouts.

101-key Keyboard

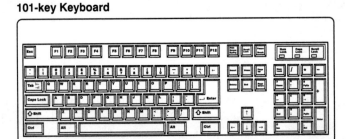

Extended Keyboard

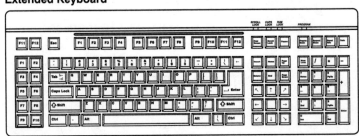

Letters

The largest grouping of keys are sometimes collectively called the typewriter keys, because the letters, numbers, and several other keys are placed in the same locations as you would find on any standard typewriter. Most keyboards color code these keys in a lighter color, although darker colored keys, such as Tab and Shift, are also found on typewriter keyboards (see fig. 1.2).

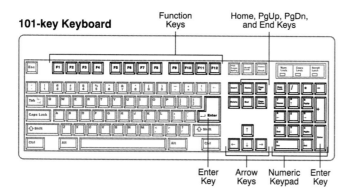

101-key Keyboard

Function Keys

Home, PgUp, PgDn, and End Keys

Enter Key — Arrow Keys — Numeric Keypad — Enter Key

Figure 1.2
Where keys are located on your keyboard.

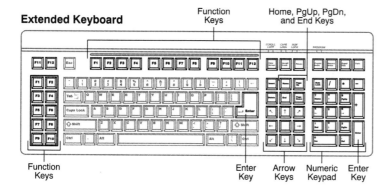

Extended Keyboard

Function Keys

Home, PgUp, PgDn, and End Keys

Function Keys

Enter Key — Arrow Keys — Numeric Keypad — Enter Key

Numbers

To the right edge of the detached keyboard is a *numeric keypad*: a group of keys resembling those found on a simple calculator. If your job entails working with lots of numbers, the numeric keypad will be in constant use. A raised dot on the 5 key helps you keep your hand in position when you can't watch the keyboard during rapid number entry.

The "F" Keys

Before the mouse became a major part of using aspects of personal computers (e.g., in the Macintosh and Windows environments), the keyboard was virtually the only way for users to communicate with the machines. Therefore, a number of extra keys simplified access to commands that might otherwise require dozens of keystrokes. For example, across the top of the 101-key keyboard, labeled F1 through F12, are *function keys*. (These keys appear in two places on the Extended keyboard.) They play a smaller role within Windows and Windows applications than in non-Windows programs, but they do offer a method of quick access to commands—*speedcuts*, we call them. Pressing the F1 key, for instance, almost always brings up some on-screen help.

More useful, however, are the Home, End, Page Up, and Page Down keys. Different software programs react to these four keys differently, but they can be speedcuts when you're doing a lot of keyboarding and have to move quickly from place to place within a document.

All keyboards have four *arrow keys* (veteran gurus might call them *cursor keys*, and Microsoft doesn't mind if you call them *direction keys*). Whatever you call them, they control the motion of something on the screen, such as a text cursor or a selected graphical item.

The Enter Key(s)

Virtually every electric typewriter made in the last 20 years (and longer for office models) has a key at the right of the keyboard that positions the carriage (or type ball) to begin typing at the left margin of the next line. In that location on the PC keyboard is the *Enter key*. Its name comes from the olden days of computing, when what you typed into the keyboard went no further than a temporary holding place; only with a press of the Enter key did the information or command actually take effect. (That's the way MS-DOS behaves, but, then, it has an ancient heritage.) While you are working on documents inside most software programs, the Enter key acts like the Return key of an electric typewriter.

Most keyboards have an additional Enter key on the numeric keypad. Its behavior is usually identical to the other Enter key but is available in the numeric pad for convenience. Be aware that some programs may assign different behavior to this Enter key.

Special Keys

Let's now focus on two special keys at the left of the typewriter keys: *Control* and *Alt* (see fig. 1.3). As with the Shift key, whose typical action is the same as on a typewriter, we use these keys in conjunction with some other key (or mouse actions). In other words, we hold down the Control or Alt key and type another.

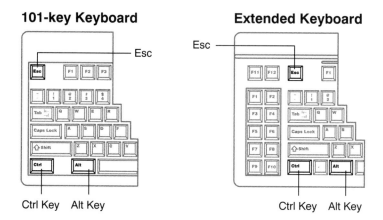

101-key Keyboard   **Extended Keyboard**

Esc

Esc

Ctrl Key   Alt Key   Ctrl Key   Alt Key

Figure 1.3
Control, Alt, and Esc key locations.

The most common application of the Control and Alt keys in Windows is for performing commands without using the mouse. It's not vital that we use these keyboard commands, but they can be speedcuts when we find ourselves running to the mouse a lot to perform the same commands.

Escape Hatch

The *Escape key* is a catch-all savior when we get into a mess and can't figure out what's going on or when we feel the need to go back to a safe place (see fig. 1.3). A press of the Escape key often cancels the last move we made. In some cases, it may take two or more presses of Escape to step our way back to safety, but it's nice to know we can bail out if needed.

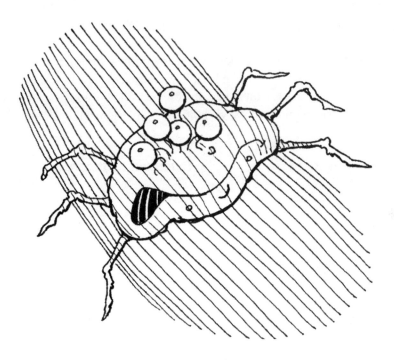

They're Out To Get Us

PC keyboards are normally very durable. They generally survive soda drenchings, animal hair infestations, and more dust than you'd really like to see. The most vulnerable spot, however, is the cable linking the keyboard to the system unit (laptop PC owners don't have to worry about this). When no key works, suspect the cable first. Be sure that it's plugged in securely to the computer's rear panel keyboard connector. If possible, try another keyboard, because keyboard cables can go bad from being bent in weird positions or kept at sharp angles over long periods.

If only one key isn't working, you know the problem is with the keyboard. Unfortunately, even though it usually means that one switch inside the keyboard is bad, most repair facilities will have to swap out the entire keyboard—for a healthy fee if it's out of warranty.

Practice

The Enter Key

With the computer off, play with entering fictional information into fictional software just to get the feel for the rhythms of entering computer information.

Enter the following information in a column, pressing the Enter key after each name:

Adams `↵Enter`
Bacon `↵Enter`
Camus `↵Enter`
Dante `↵Enter`
Eliot `↵Enter`
Faulkner `↵Enter`

Figure 1.4 shows a printout of the Enter key practice session.

Adams
Bacon
Camus
Dante
Eliot
Faulkner

Figure 1.4
The results of your practice session.

The Tab Key

Enter the following information in a three-column format, pressing Tab after the first and second names and Enter at the end of each line:

Last `Tab⇥` First `Tab⇥` Title `↵Enter`
Machiavelli `Tab⇥` Niccolo `Tab⇥` The Prince `↵Enter`
Nietzche `Tab⇥` Friedrich `Tab⇥` Beyond Good and Evil `↵Enter`
O'Neill `Tab⇥` Eugene `Tab⇥` Mourning Becomes Electra `↵Enter`
Paine `Tab⇥` Thomas `Tab⇥` The Age of Reason `↵Enter`
Rabelais `Tab⇥` Francois `Tab⇥` Gargantua and Pantagruel `↵Enter`
Santayana `Tab⇥` George `Tab⇥` Scepticism and Animal Faith `↵Enter`

A printout of this session is shown in figure 1.5.

Figure 1.5

The results of the Tab key practice session.

Last	First	Title
Machiavelli	Niccolo	The Prince
Nietzche	Friedrich	Beyond Good and Evil
O'Neill	Eugene	Mourning Becomes Electra
Paine	Thomas	The Age of Reason
Rabelais	Francois	Gargantua and Pantagruel
Santayana	George	Scepticism and Animal Faith

The Control Key

Common commands issued with the Control key are Ctrl-X, Ctrl-C, and Ctrl-V, all of which are on the left side of the keyboard. Developing a one-handed technique is valuable (but not crucial).

1. Issue a Ctrl-C with your left hand by pressing the Control key with your pinkie and the C key with your left index finger.

2. Say Control-C aloud to associate the physical action with the command.

3. Release all keys and cycle through these three commands (Ctrl-X, -C, and -V) at least 10 times, saying the word "Control" and the letter out loud as you press the letter.

The Alt Key

One helpful Alt key combination—Alt-Tab—lets us instantly switch among programs that are open at any moment. By holding down the Alt key and typing the Tab key repeatedly, Windows displays the name of the next program in the sequence of open programs. Releasing the Alt key makes the selected program the active one on the screen.

Get used to the feel of cycling through your Windows applications. Hold down the Alt key and press the Tab key three times. Then release the Alt key. Repeat this action 10 times.

Summary

We've seen how the basic layout of the PC keyboard combines familiar typewriter keyboards, calculator keyboards, and some special keys. Special keys commonly used in Windows are Escape, Control, and Alt, but the mouse makes these keys less important than they are under MS-DOS.

Exorcises

1. How many function keys are there on the PC keyboard?

2. After issuing a command, the screen presents a message that sounds as if continuing may do something you're not sure of. One of the choices on the screen says `Cancel`. Which key would you press to get out of this pickle?

   a. Alt

   b. Control

   c. Escape

   d. F1

3. A software manual suggests that you try typing Alt-Shift-F5. What exactly does this mean you should do?

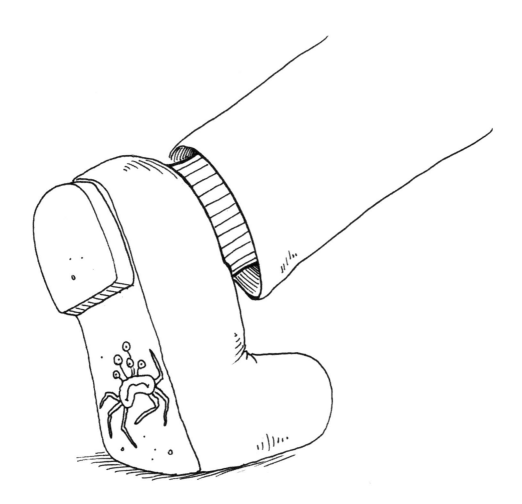

2nd Encounter

Powering Up the PC and Windows

Goal

Learn what happens when you turn on your PC and how to get Windows running if it doesn't run automatically.

What You Will Need

Computer turned off.

Terms of Enfearment

booting   "C" prompt
startup   desktop
MS-DOS
MS-DOS Shell

Briefing
Finding the Switch

The first time you sit before your PC, it may not be clear how to turn the darned thing on. After all, many PCs don't have a big ON/OFF or Power switch staring you in the face. Desktop PCs come in all shapes and sizes. Sometimes, a power button or switch is plainly visible on the front panel. If not, you may have to search the side or rear panels for the switch.

What Happens Next?

Getting the computer to begin doing its thing is known by a couple of jargon terms. The most arcane is called *booting* the computer. No, not like kicking it in the butt with your boot. The term derives from the more formal term, bootstrap, which, in turn, came from the idea that the hunk of wires and components pulls itself up by its bootstraps to start acting like a computer.

When you turn on the machine, it goes through an automatic process that can last a minute or so. The first task it performs is a quick check of some of the machine's innards. You may see evidence on the screen of the computer performing a self-test of its internal memory (see fig. 2.1). If everything is OK, you'll hear a tone or chord come through the speaker. You want to hear this sound every time.

Figure 2.1
Your PC may check its memory while starting up.

```
Copyright 1993, Giant Computer Corporation, Inc.

MEMORY TEST 4096K
```

The Ugly Part

Inside, the computer looks for further instructions to become the kind of computer you bought it for. These instructions are contained in software formally called *MS-DOS*. Most users call it *DOS* (rhymes with boss). The letters stand for Microsoft Disk Operating System (yikes!), but all you need to know about DOS at this point is that it gives people a measure of control over the way information is stored and organized in a PC.

As the PC gets DOS up and running, the video screen may display a number of complex-looking messages. On a fast PC, they may scroll by so quickly that you can't read them. All the better! Those messages describe some of the automatic processes that are loaded specifically into your PC. Other users probably have different sets of processes loaded into their machines, depending on who originally set up the machine or who has monkeyed with it since then.

Where Are You?

Because there's no way for me to know how your PC has been set up to boot, I can only assume that you are in one of four places after everything seems to settle down:

- In Microsoft Windows. You would have seen the Microsoft Windows logo appear as part of the booting process.

- In a program called *MS-DOS Shell*. Just because there are window-like things on the screen doesn't mean you're in the real Windows.

- Some other menu or shell program installed by the last person to muck around with your PC.

- In plain old DOS with the cursor blinking after a line of text on the screen that looks something like C:> or C:\>. This is called the *C:> prompt* (pronounced see-prompt).

If booting your PC takes you straightaway into Windows, you're in luck. Although Windows requires that MS-DOS be running on your PC, it also shields you from the complex commands and extra work that DOS requires. You can skip ahead to the 3rd Encounter.

MS-DOS Shell—Neanderthal Windows

The DOS Shell (which comes with DOS 5.0 and up) attempts to put a friendly face on MS-DOS and is indeed a helpful tool when either your PC doesn't have the horsepower needed to run Windows or when the programs you must use do not work under Windows. For our purposes here, however, it will be easiest to take advantage of a command indicated on the bottom of the DOS Shell screen:

```
Shift + F9 Command Prompt.
```

Hold down the Shift key and press the F9 function key (see fig. 2.2). This key combination brings you to the C:\> prompt (the "C" does not stand for "command"—any DOS prompt followed by the ">" is a command prompt).

Figure 2.2

MS-DOS Shell. We want the command prompt (Shift-F9).

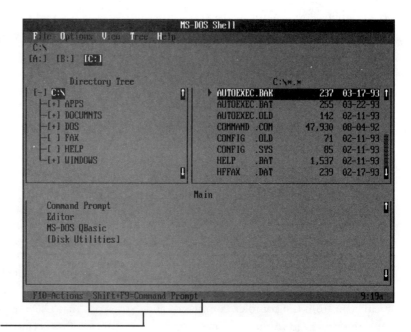

Instructions for command prompt

If someone else has set up a Main menu or other shell around DOS for your PC, there's no way of telling how you may have to proceed for now. Unless there is an obvious action that indicates it starts Windows, look for a command that lets you "exit to DOS" or view the "command prompt."

See the Win

Unless you've used DOS before, that `C:\>` prompt is probably quite a mystery. You'll learn more about it later, but for now it's enough to know that this prompt awaits a command. Whatever command you type will be sent to the hard disk, where, hopefully, an identically named program is there to respond to our command.

The command that starts Windows is the three-letter shortcut, **win** (see fig. 2.3). This command, like all commands in DOS, must be followed by a press of the Enter key to send the command.

```
C:\>win
```

Figure 2.3
Type win at the DOS prompt and press the Enter key.

Following the Microsoft Windows banner shown in figure 2.4 (to keep you company while Windows sets itself up), you see the primary Windows screen, which is called the *desktop*. We'll learn about the desktop in the next lesson (see fig. 3.1).

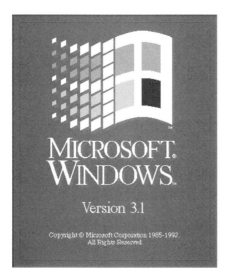

Figure 2.4
The Microsoft Windows banner.

They're Out To Get Us

The startup process on a PC and Windows is perhaps the most likely place you'll encounter problems that seem insurmountable. The problems will be due to things as innocuous as a loose cable to the extremely rare, yet harrowing, damaged hard disk. I've reserved a special encounter (19th) on how to diagnose and get help for such problems.

When absolutely nothing happens, look to the obvious problem that electric power is not reaching the PC (or the laptop's battery has run down). Either the power cable isn't connected, or it's plugged into a power outlet that doesn't have power (perhaps the outlet is controlled by a light switch that is off).

If you've just purchased your PC and it doesn't start, make it the responsibility of the seller (be it dealer or individual) to get the machine functioning properly. If you're in a corporate environment, contact the technical support person for help in making sure that the computer turns on properly. Lastly, if you're stuck with no one to turn to for help, you can jump ahead to the first part of the 19th Encounter and try working your way through. Chances are that the problem for a newly acquired machine is a simple one that won't be technically taxing.

If your PC doesn't automatically start up in Windows, it's going to be a pain in the neck going through all the steps I described earlier each time you turn on the machine and want to use Windows. Instructing your PC to run Windows during startup is not a complex task but is daunting for newcomers to DOS. If you have someone to turn to for help, ask him or her to do the following for you: "Modify my autoexec batch file to run Windows." You'll sound like a pro, even though you may not have a clue what an autoexec (pronounced au-to-eggs-ECK) batch file is.

Practice

Power On, Dude

For the 99.99 percent of you who are working your way through this lesson, your PC will turn on properly. It's important that you listen and watch carefully as the startup process progresses.

1. If your PC has an external video monitor, turn its power switch on. If the monitor's power cord is plugged into the PC's system unit, nothing should happen yet.

2. Using the "Briefing" as a guide, locate, *but do not yet flip*, the power switch for your PC.

3. With all your senses poised for input, turn on the power switch and watch the screen carefully.

Starting Windows

1. If your PC didn't automatically start Windows, use the "Briefing" section as a guide to reach the C:\> DOS command prompt.

2. Type *win* and press the Enter key.

3. Unless you already know how to get out of Windows, leave it and your PC running for the next few lessons. (They won't take long.)

Summary

We've learned how to start up a PC and some fundamentals of MS-DOS along the way. Importantly, we've seen that Windows is software that runs atop MS-DOS, not in place of it.

Exorcises

1. Switching on the PC is called _____ the computer.

2. Instructions for turning the computer's components into a device we can use are contained in the disk operating system, whose commercial name is _____.

3. If you turn on your computer and see, after all other activity, the characters `C:\>`, this is called the _____.

What You See on the Screen

Goal

Recognize the elements of the basic Windows screen.

What You Will Need

Your PC turned on and Windows running.

Terms of Enfearment

hard disk
Program Manager
window
pointer
menu bar
group icon
program item icon

Briefing

Your PC remembers things from session to session because all information you type or draw is stored on the device known as the *hard disk* (equivalent terms: *hard drive* and *fixed disk*). Yes, it actually rotates like a record or compact disc and can store a large amount of information in a relatively small space. A future encounter explores what's actually on the hard disk and how we manage stuff on it, but for now, all we need to know is that it is an important repository for information and programs that let the PC act as a word processor, spreadsheet, or whatever else we want it to do.

What win Does

The win command that starts Windows is not the actual Windows software we'll get our hands on for the rest of our Window-using lives. Instead, the win program (its full name is win.com) pokes around the PC to see how much memory it has, what kind of video display it uses, and many other hidden tasks important to Windows' innards. Other than the Windows logo, the only other visible result of the win program is the underlying screen space we see a lot of the time. This area is called the desktop and acts just like the top of a real working desk. All action on a real desk occurs in layers of papers and folders on top of it; all Windows action occurs in layers atop the Windows desktop. The Windows desktop may not be oak or rosewood, but it means as much business as any executive desktop you'll ever see.

One of win's last tasks is to start a Windows module with which we interact. Unless your copy of Windows has been adjusted otherwise, the module that comes on the screen is called the *Program Manager* (see fig. 3.1).

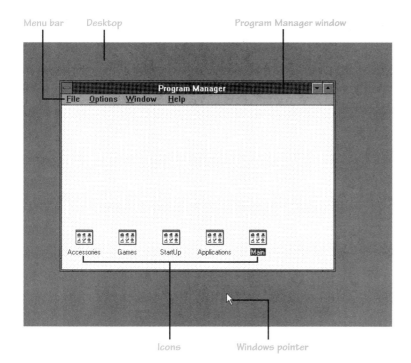

Figure 3.1
*The Windows
desktop, showing the
Program Manager
window.*

Icons   Windows pointer

Our First Window

Almost everything that happens while using Windows occurs in large
rectangular screen elements called—ta da—*windows.* In some cases, such as
the Program Manager window, the information contained in a window is
small enough so that we can see it all at a glance; other times, the window
(or our video monitor) isn't large enough to see everything contained in the
window, so we have to shift the contents around (called scrolling, covered
later). Windows are resizable and movable.

Desktop Elements

Because it is usually vital to point to something on the Windows screen to
issue a command or say the equivalent of "I want to work with this thing

here," a *pointer* is always visible on the screen (see fig. 3.1). In the next encounter, we'll see how to control that pointer.

Inside the Program Manager window are two elements we'll use constantly: a menu bar and icons.

Across the top of the Program Manager window (and just below the window's name) is the *menu bar*. We'll cover this in detail in the 5th Encounter. Suffice it to say that the menu bar is where we issue commands to make many things happen inside the window.

Icons appear everywhere throughout Windows. They are symbols that represent something more tangible, such as documents, programs, or windows full of items. Later, we'll see how to use the mouse to bring an icon's contents to life and how to use icons as speedcuts to get to our work.

What Program Manager Does

The name, Program Manager, may be an unfortunate choice, because it implies that it manages programs. In truth, we're the ones who manage programs with the help of the Program Manager.

By making the Program Manager the module that comes up on screen in a factory-fresh copy of Windows, it's clear that Microsoft expects us to use the Program Manager as the focal point of Windows activity. Used correctly, the Program Manager provides an uncluttered hub for us to start and switch among programs we use to get our work done.

Program Manager Icons

It's easy to get confused about Program Manager icons because they don't represent programs. Rather, each icon represents another window, which can contain one or more icons for programs. As a result, the icons in the Program Manager window are called *group icons*. For example, one group automatically installed by Windows is called Accessories. Inside this group are *program item icons*, each of which represents an accessory program supplied by Windows (see fig. 3.2). We'll see how to open up these groups to see and arrange their contents in the 9th Encounter.

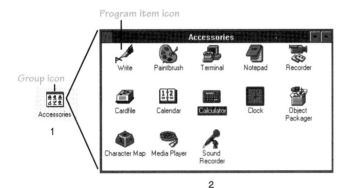

2

Figure 3.2

The Accessories group icon (1) and the program item icons it contains (2).

From the Real World

Because the Program Manager isn't a clear metaphor of real-world things most of us work with every day, let's set up a scenario that illustrates how effective the Program Manager can be.

Imagine that you manage a department of 10 specialists. One person is a good writer, another a great illustrator, yet another knows how the company filing system works, and so on. As you've gotten to know the strengths and weaknesses of each individual, you begin thinking of various combinations of them as informal teams. For one kind of project that comes your way, you consider one team consisting of the writer, illustrator, and typist as a solid group; for another kind of project, the writer, photographer, and researcher are the perfect group.

In your mind, each specialist has a separate identity but is also a part of one or more groups. For many occasions, it is easier to think of the group as an entity and to pull the group's strings (isn't that what bosses do?).

In the Program Manager Window

Pulling those group strings is what we do in the Program Manager. We can assign a pet name to any group and decide which specialists (programs) go into each group. For example, the Windows folks at Microsoft decided to help us along by providing a group of simple programs that it calls accessories (things like an on-screen calculator, card filer, and Notepad). At the outset, Microsoft puts program item icons for these programs into an Accessories group.

Just because Windows comes this way doesn't mean that the Accessories group or its program items are cast in stone. We have the freedom to reorganize these program items into other groups if we like, to eliminate the Accessories group, or to place copies of a program item in as many groups as makes sense for us in the way we use those programs. Just like the manager shuffles people and teams for a project.

The problem with this whole system is that, in practice, the Program Manager places unnecessary steps between us and accomplishing real work in Windows (see fig. 3.3). As a result, I devote the 9th Encounter to setting up the Program Manager for ultimate simplicity and practicality.

Figure 3.3
One of unlimited alternatives to Program Manager organization.

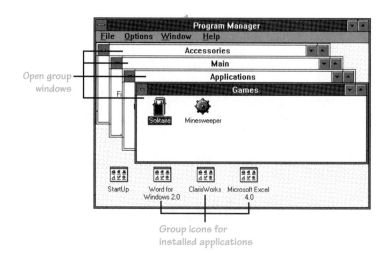

They're Out To Get Us

If anything is going to confuse you about your first explorations around the desktop and Program Manager, it will be caused by someone else who has been fiddling around with your PC (see fig. 3.4). For instance, it is possible to instruct Windows to automatically start one or more programs when Windows starts up. Those programs can be run in what Windows calls minimized mode—in which case actual program icons appear at the very bottom of the desktop (i.e., not in the Program Manager window). I'll even recommend automating the startup process later on for programs you use all the time. But, at first, it doesn't correspond to what you've been seeing in the book. Don't worry about any visual discrepancies for the moment.

Someone may have altered the desktop pattern. Although Windows allows easy desktop pattern selections from a preset library of *wallpaper* designs (see the 16th Encounter), it is equally possible that a custom pattern has been put into your machine. Again, there's nothing to worry about. A colorful pattern may slow down an already slow machine, and it may take up some system resources better used by your programs, but you can make that determination later.

Figure 3.4
Your initial desktop may have other stuff showing that was set up by a previous user.

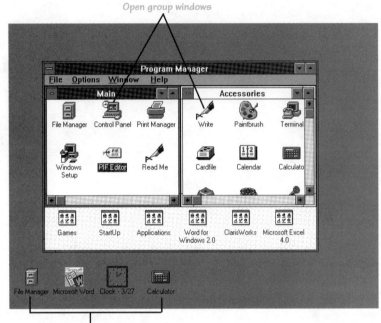

Open group windows

Programs set up to appear as icons on the desktop.

Practice

Getting To Know You

In this get-acquainted encounter, you simply use your finger to point to each of the major elements that Windows presents to the screen and say its name aloud. Point at (but keep your finger off the screen if you can) the following items and say their names. Go through all items until you can point to all five items and name them without referring to the illustrations or text earlier in this encounter.

desktop
window
menu bar
pointer
group icon

Summary

I introduced the Windows desktop and Program Manager display elements. These elements are important building blocks for working with Windows minute-by-minute.

Exorcises

1. The program that runs when we start Windows is called
   _____.

2. A hallmark of the Windows display is its real-world metaphor to a
   _____, which, by no surprise on Windows is called
   _____.

3. Virtually all action we perform in Windows takes place in
   _____.

Getting Used to the Mouse

Goal

Gain confidence and coordination controlling the pointer with the mouse; understand the use of the left mouse button and standard mouse actions.

What You Will Need

PC turned on and Windows running.

Terms of Enfearment

mouse	dragging
mouse button	drag-and-drop
clicking	double-click
selecting	

Briefing

Hello, Mr. Mouse

When the Apple Macintosh computer first appeared in 1984, the mouse made its way into the mainstream of personal computing. Previously used only on very expensive computers for special graphics purposes, the mouse—a cigarette-pack sized device tethered to the computer—is as important to controlling Windows as the keyboard.

Although it is possible to use Windows exclusively from the keyboard, it is very clumsy to do so—like hitching a horse to a car and expecting to merge into highway traffic. In fact, some of the screen and menu clutter we'll encounter exists only because Windows accommodates keyboard-only users. This book assumes that you'll be using a mouse (or mouse equivalent) with Windows. You do want to learn the most painless way of using Windows, don't you?

Moving the Screen Pointer

In the last encounter, we saw the pointer on the screen. The mouse is what we use to move the pointer around the screen. The direction of pointer movement corresponds to the direction in which we move the mouse: in straight lines, diagonals, or even circles if we like (see fig. 4.1). Windows won't let us move the pointer entirely off the screen. If you should lose sight of the pointer, jiggle the mouse a bit until you see something—the pointer—move.

The most effective way to hold the mouse is to cover it with your hand so that it fills your palm; your thumb should be against one side, and your middle, ring, and pinkie fingers should grab the other side. Your index finger should be free to rest atop the leftmost rectangle near the mouse cord. This is one of the *mouse buttons*, and you use your index finger to press down and release it—an action called *clicking* (you can usually hear an internal switch click when you press and release the button). The other button (or buttons, if you have a three-button mouse) doesn't do anything in Windows but may perform specific operations inside programs. Therefore, unless I note otherwise, whenever I refer to the mouse button, I mean the *left* mouse button.

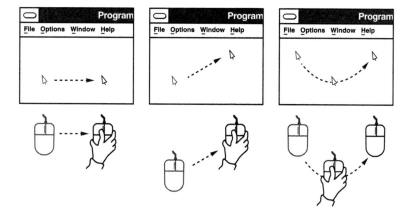

Figure 4.1
Pointer motion on the screen desktop is identical to mouse motion on the physical desk.

Clicking the Mouse Button

Just moving the pointer around the screen usually doesn't invoke any actions. That's what the mouse button is for.

If we position the pointer atop an icon on the screen and click the mouse button, something usually happens. Most commonly, the icon we clicked becomes active (the icon name changes color or is highlighted as shown in fig. 4.2). This is how we select one item from all the others in a window so that we can then issue some command to affect that item. When an instruction tells you to click on an item, position the pointer atop the item, press the mouse button, and release it. Highlighting an item like this is also called *selecting* the item. The next instruction probably acts on that selected item.

Figure 4.2
Clicking an icon selects it, as denoted by the change in color around the icon's name.

Highlighted name means the icon is selected.

On a Roll

The next important action we accomplish with the mouse is a combination of two actions we've already covered: clicking the mouse (while holding the mouse button down) *and* moving the mouse and its pointer (see fig. 4.3). Contrary to the old joke, even people who deem themselves as uncoordinated *can* chew gum and walk at the same time. Our action here is no more complex than holding and sliding an object across a table without picking it up. The formal term for this action is *clicking and dragging*—or just dragging (which assumes, correctly, that we can't drag an item unless we have clicked and held it first). It's far easier than rubbing your tummy and patting your head at the same time.

Figure 4.3
Clicking and dragging moves an icon around the screen.

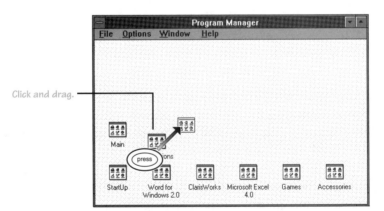

In addition to just moving things around by clicking and dragging, some actions we can take with icons involve dragging one item to another item (see fig. 4.4). As we'll see later, this is one way to shift an item from one container to another. This kind of action is magic compared to real life, because it lets us essentially drag a document on top of a folder, and the document zips inside the folder.

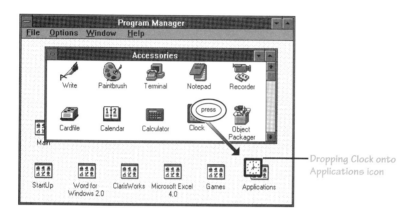

Figure 4.4
Dragging an item from one window to an icon representing another window. Just dropping it on the group icon moves it to that group.

Dropping Clock onto Applications icon

Windows visually guides us to know when we're dragging an item to a valid destination. The item we're dragging turns into an international "No" sign whenever the underlying window or desktop area won't accept whatever it is we're dragging (see fig. 4.5). If the area is valid, the icon stays in its original form.

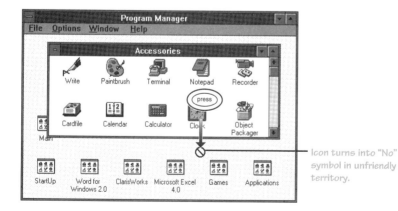

Figure 4.5
Dragging a program item to the desktop turns the icon into the "No" symbol.

Icon turns into "No" symbol in unfriendly territory.

In other parts of Windows, an additional clue lets us know when we've dragged the item atop another item that accepts it: the destination item highlights with a surrounding rectangle as shown in figure 4.6: it is ready to accept the drop (i.e., release of the mouse button). The *drag and drop* concept not only makes many aspects of Windows easy to manage, but it is also gaining popularity inside Windows programs.

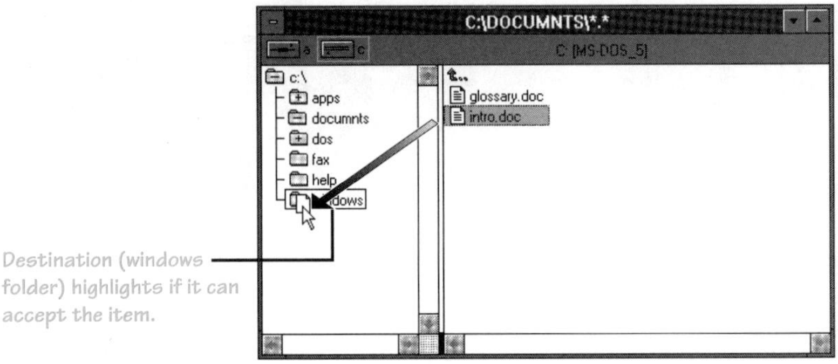

Figure 4.6

Elsewhere in Windows, the destination highlights when it's ready to accept a drop.

Destination (windows folder) highlights if it can accept the item.

Click-Click

The last mouse action I'll cover here—the *double-click*—is actually a speedcut to otherwise laborious actions. A double-click consists of nothing more than two quickly spaced clicks of the mouse button. A double-click atop an icon is generally the way to bring that icon alive (see fig. 4.7). For example, double-clicking on a Program Manager group icon zooms open that group's window so that you see some or all of its contents; double-clicking a program's icon starts that program; in the File Manager (another part of Windows you'll meet soon), double-clicking on a folder icon opens up that folder. All of these actions could be carried out more laboriously by single clicking—selecting—the icon and then issuing a command from the menu bar. Double-clicking is much faster and should become natural to you in a short time.

How the mouse and buttons respond to the speed of our actions is modifiable. We'll learn more about this in the 16th Encounter, but take comfort in knowing that we can adjust how quickly the pointer reacts to quick rolling of the mouse and double clicks.

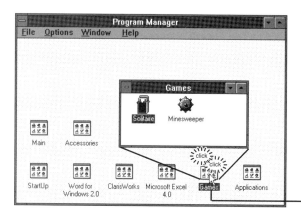

Figure 4.7
Double-clicking an icon opens it up, such as this group window from a double-click of its icon.

The Mouse and Desk Space

Early mousers will encounter those moments when there isn't enough desk to finish moving the pointer or dragging an item on the screen. What to do, what to do! Remember that the pointer responds to motion of the little roller under the mouse. If we pick up the mouse and wave it in the air, the roller doesn't move, so the pointer doesn't either. Therefore, we can literally pick up the mouse from the desk surface and place it where we'll have more space to finish the movement.

If you find, however, that you are doing a lot of this, it probably means that you should adjust the mouse motion (called tracking), which I cover in the 16th Encounter.

They're Out To Get Us

When the mouse doesn't seem to work, a couple of things could be going on. The simplest is that the mouse isn't connected properly. A mouse is usually connected to the serial port called COM1; on more recent machines, especially laptop computers, there is a separate mouse port. The mouse must be connected to your PC *before* you start Windows, or Windows probably won't recognize the mouse—you won't see a pointer on the screen.

Sometimes, special software for your mouse is missing. Windows automatically recognizes a wide variety of mouse brands and models, but you should install the software that comes with your mouse. This software is system-level stuff, which gets loaded into the PC every subsequent booting.

If the mouse has been working fine during a Windows session but then suddenly stops, you have a frozen pointer—a good chance that the computer or program has locked up.

Mouse innards can get dirty (animal hair is a primary enemy), and the balls may not spin freely or smoothly. It's then time to remove and clean the roller balls as described in the user's guide that came with your mouse.

Practice

Roll, Roll, Roll Your Mouse

Get the feel of how the pointer responds to mouse movement by performing the following pointer motions:

a. Move the pointer a couple of inches on the screen back and forth horizontally.

b. Do the same vertically.

c. Try moving the pointer a short distance along a diagonal.

d. With the pointer on the left side of the screen, *slowly* move the mouse until the pointer is touching the right side of the screen. If you are using a mouse and run out of desk space, pick up the mouse and position it back on the left of the space to continue the pointer's journey across the screen.

e. With the pointer on the right side of the screen, move the mouse *quickly* until the pointer is touching the left side of the screen. How quickly it moves (it may do it in much less space than before) depends on an internal setting we'll adjust in a later encounter.

Clicking

Now we'll practice single clicking.

a. Click once on the Main group icon in the Program Manager window. For now, ignore the menu that pops up but pay close attention to how the icon name highlights to distinguish it from others in the window.

b. Click once on the Accessories group icon. The previously selected item is no longer selected.

c. Click once on the white space of the Program Manager window surrounding the icons. The menu goes away, but the icon stays highlighted. One item is always highlighted in the Program Manager window.

Dragging

1. Click and drag a group icon from the bottom of the window to a location near the top of the window. Release the mouse button to see the icon's name reappear.

2. Try to drag this icon outside the Program Manager window. These icons exist only in the Program Manager window and cannot be dragged outside. This isn't true throughout Windows but does apply to Program Manager group icons.

3. Click and drag the icon back to its original spot (the exact location isn't critical).

Double-Clicking

Double-click the Main group icon. If no window had been open before, one will zoom out of the icon, revealing several more icons.

Drag and Drop

1. Locate the program item icon labeled Read Me and click it once to select it.

2. Without releasing the mouse button until I say so, first drag the icon outside the Main window but still within the white space of the Program Manager window. Notice how the icon turns into the "No" sign, meaning that nothing will happen if you try to drop the item in that spot.

3. Continue dragging the item, but this time, drag it outside the Program Manager window to the desktop area. The icon stays as the No sign, because this isn't the place for a program item icon.

4. Release the mouse button. Nothing has happened to the item you dragged.

5. Drag the Read Me icon again, but this time, roll it around the Program Manager window so that it touches some of the other group icons in the window. Notice that the icon alternates between the No sign and its original art. Don't do it now, but if you were to release the mouse button when the icon is atop one of the group icons, you would be dropping the item into that group window.

6. Drag the item back to its original position in the Main window and release the mouse button.

Summary

By learning the primary actions of the mouse, we've completed a survey of the physical means of interacting with the computer—including the keyboard from the previous encounter. Important concepts for the mouse include clicking to select an item, dragging an item across the screen, double-clicking an item, and dragging and dropping one item onto another.

Exorcises

1. When you click on an item, you also _____ that item.

2. Describe the three primary physical actions involved with dragging an item from one place to another.

3. If you seen an icon on the screen, what would you do to see what it can do or what it contains?

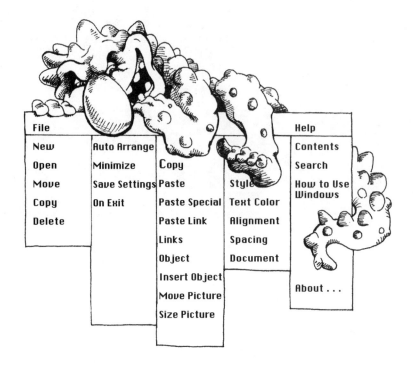

File				Help
New	Auto Arrange	Copy		Contents
Open	Minimize	Paste	Style	Search
Move	Save Settings	Paste Special	Text Color	How to Use Windows
Copy	On Exit	Paste Link	Alignment	
Delete		Links	Spacing	
		Object	Document	
		Insert Object		About . . .
		Move Picture		
		Size Picture		

5th Encounter

Controlling the Machine

Goal

Learn to rely on the menu bar as the first place to look for what to do next.

What You Will Need

PC turned on with Windows running

Terms of Enfearment

drop-down menu	dimmed item
dialog box	keyboard equivalents
File Menu	cascading menus
Edit Menu	window control menu
Help menu	

Briefing

What's Next?

We've seen how to get something to happen on the Windows screen by double-clicking items or dragging them around. But how do we get down to some real work? What is the machine capable of doing at any given moment?

The primary communication path between us and Windows is via menus—lists of things we can do within a window. When you don't know what to do next, the best place to look is the menus in the hope of finding something there that rings a bell.

Windows menus—in the menu bar—are called *drop-down menus*, because when we click on a menu name, a list of choices drops down on the screen (although they sometimes drop up). Each menu has a name that indicates the category of commands in that menu. The leftmost menu in the Program Manager window (also of virtually every window you'll see in Windows) is the File menu (see fig. 5.1).

Figure 5.1

The Program Manager menu bar contains four menus: File, Options, Window, and Help.

Menus for this window

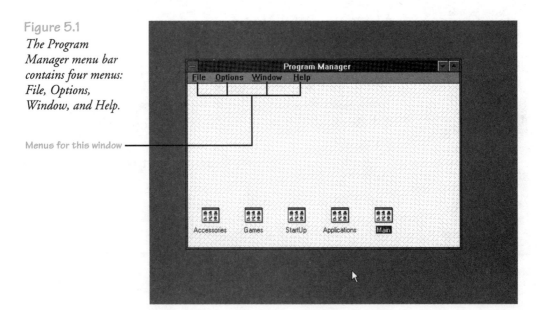

Check Out a Menu

To view a menu's contents, summon your click experience. First, position the pointer atop the menu name. Then click the mouse button (see fig. 5.2). To close the menu without making a choice, click anywhere outside the menu or on the menu name again. If you click on another menu name to close one menu, the second menu's list appears.

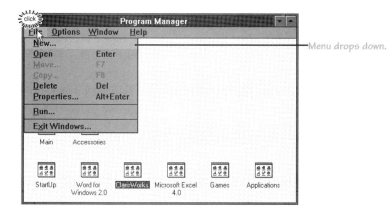

Figure 5.2
Click on a menu, and the menu drops down for your perusal.

To check out several menus with the minimum of mouse clicks, we can scan each menu in turn by dragging slowly across the menu bar (see fig. 5.3). Dragging the pointer to another menu rolls up the first menu and drops down the next.

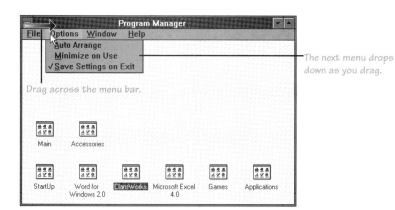

Figure 5.3
Click and slowly drag across the menu bar to view contents of all menus.

Make a Choice

Although we can click a menu to drop it down and then click on an item in the menu to choose that action, it is more efficient to do it all with a single click-and-drag (see fig. 5.4). Click and hold the menu open; then drag down the menu. As the pointer touches each item in the menu, that item highlights to confirm to us which item is currently selected. We can drag up and down the menu. If the pointer goes *outside* the bounds of the pulled down menu, no item will be selected—releasing the mouse button now is another way to let the menu roll up without taking any action.

Figure 5.4
*Click and drag down
a menu to choose an
item.*

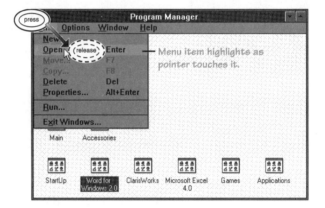

Longer menus usually divide items into logical groups. A dividing line separates the groups and does not highlight as the pointer drags over it (see fig. 5.5).

Figure 5.5
*Two dividing lines
separate this menu
into three groups.*

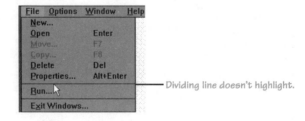

When you've found a menu item that you want, make sure that it is selected and release the mouse button.

Dot-Dot-Dot...

Not all menu selections take immediate actions when we choose them. When chosen, a menu item that ends with three dots (called an ellipsis) will display a *dialog box* (see fig. 5.6). Such dialog boxes can contain just about anything, but they always have a Cancel button, OK button, or other control, which lets us close the dialog box to return to the exact state we were in before we pulled down the original menu.

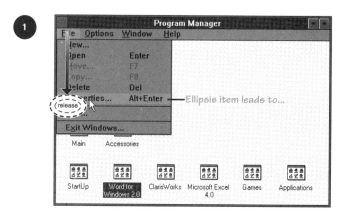

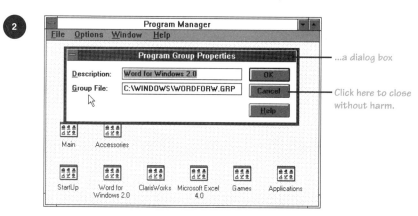

Figure 5.6
Choosing the Properties command leads to the Properties dialog box, which we can put away by clicking the Cancel button.

Standard Menus

Each program you run in Windows (like the Program Manager) has its own menu bar within its window. The menu bar may have anywhere from one to about a dozen menus (the latter making for quite an intimidating menu bar). When you start using application programs, you'll see some consistency of menus, making it easier for you to switch freely between applications without having to recollect an entirely new method of performing common functions.

A few menus, however, are usually present in programs, even if their contents change from program to program. These are called the *File, Edit,* and *Help* menus (see fig. 5.7). The File and Edit menus are the first ones on the left, and the Help menu tends to be the rightmost menu. Any additional menus (some small programs have no additional menus) fill in between the Edit and Help menus. Their names, contents, and functions are determined solely by the program.

Figure 5.7

Menu bars from three different programs all have File, Edit, and Help menus.

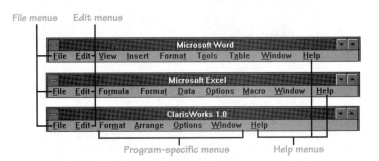

Dim, But Not Dumb

From time to time, you will encounter menus or items in a menu that appear grayed-out. These are said to be *dimmed* (see fig. 5.8). We can obviously view a dimmed item to see what it says, but in no way can we select it with the pointer. A dimmed item is not available.

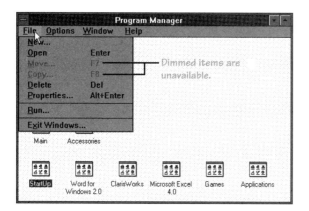

Figure 5.8
A menu with two dimmed items, which don't highlight.

When we see a dimmed item, it means that something else isn't set properly for that menu item to mean anything. For example, in the Program Manager, if we click on a group icon, two items in the Program Manager's File menu (Move and Size) are dimmed, because they don't apply to group icons. If we then click on a program item icon inside a group, all File menu items are active (see fig. 5.9). We don't have to know exactly what those Move and Size menu items do to know that they don't affect group icons.

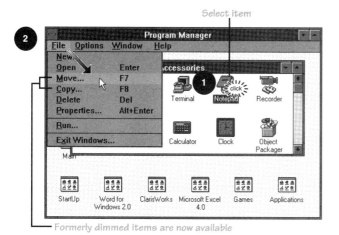

Figure 5.9
The same menu with relevant items already selected: the dimmed items are now active.

Look Ma, No Mouse!

Many menu commands can be activated from the keyboard, completely bypassing the menus. Menu items followed by legends such as F10, Alt+F4, Ctrl+X, or Ctrl+Shift+F5 have *keyboard equivalents* (see fig. 5.10). Single key equivalents—usually one of the Function keys—are simple enough to perform. The others indicate that we need to hold down one or more special keys before typing the last key. Thus, with Shift+Ctrl+R, we press and hold both the Control and Shift keys before pressing the R key. By doing so, we accomplish the same as pulling down the menu with the mouse, selecting the item, and releasing the mouse button. Keyboard equivalents are provided expressly as speedcuts.

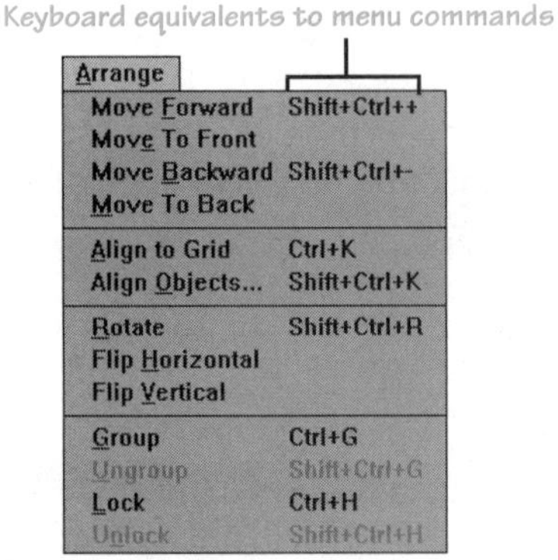

Figure 5.10

A menu with a proliferation of keyboard equivalents.

Keyboard equivalents to menu commands

Arrange	
Move Forward	Shift+Ctrl++
Move To Front	
Move Backward	Shift+Ctrl+-
Move To Back	
Align to Grid	Ctrl+K
Align Objects...	Shift+Ctrl+K
Rotate	Shift+Ctrl+R
Flip Horizontal	
Flip Vertical	
Group	Ctrl+G
Ungroup	Shift+Ctrl+G
Lock	Ctrl+H
Unlock	Shift+Ctrl+H

You don't have to bother learning them. To make them easier to work into your routine, however, most Windows programs share a number of command-key equivalents for common operations:

Key(s)	Menu Command	What It Does
Ctrl+X	Cut	Deletes a selected item.
Ctrl+C	Copy	Stores a copy of a selected item in memory.
Ctrl+V	Paste	Inserts an item from memory.

Key(s)	Menu Command	What It Does
Ctrl+Z	Undo	Restores the state just prior to the last action.
Alt+F4	Exit	Closes down the program.

A Menu's Menu

You will likely encounter in some programs an additional menu element: a right-facing triangle along the right edge of a menu (see fig. 5.11). Newcomers find these *cascading menus* tricky, because they take a bit of careful mousing to access successfully (see fig. 5.12). When we drag the pointer through a cascading menu item, a submenu appears to the right of the main menu. To select an item in the submenu, the trick is to drag the pointer horizontally to the right until the pointer starts highlighting items. Then we can drag vertically within the submenu to make our selection. If we let the pointer slide back into the main menu, the submenu disappears, and we'll have to do that tricky part again. Experienced Windows users either swear by them or at them, but when cascading menus are built into a program, we all have to use them.

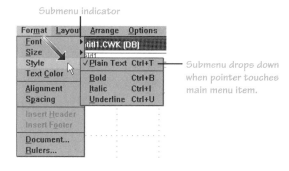

Figure 5.11

A menu item followed by a right-facing arrow means that a submenu appears when selected.

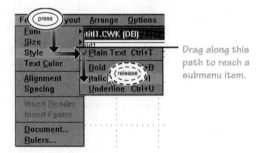

Figure 5.12
Choosing an item in
a cascading menu
can take some tricky
mouse work or lots of
clicks.

Look Ma, No Mouse—At All!

Yes, it's possible to do everything in Windows without a mouse, including
pull down menus and make selections. All you have to remember is how to
gain access to the menu bar from the keyboard: the Alt key. Press it once,
and the leftmost menu highlights. After that, use arrow keys and/or the
underlined letters you see in the menu bar and menus (sometimes the letters
are not the first character of the command, because the letter is taken by a
preceding menu item) to navigate through and select menu items. If you use
the arrow keys to highlight a command, press the Enter key to make the
choice. To move from one Program Group to another, you can use the Ctrl
and Tab key combination.

Although you should get used to the mouse as much as possible, there's
nothing preventing you from viewing these manual menu actions as keyboard equivalent commands, even if they display all kinds of menus and
generally require more keystrokes and human memory. You should use
whatever works best for you, including combinations of mouse, keyboard
equivalents, and keyboard menus.

Menu Turn-Off

When you operate inside Windows all day, it's easy to forget that Windows
is a program, not the basic computer itself. Thus, it's best to shut down
Windows before switching off the PC. This allows Windows to make sure
that all changes to documents are saved and that the Windows desktop
status is preserved for you tomorrow (if so desired).

To shut down Windows, we need to access a menu that we haven't acknowledged quite yet, even though you may have encountered it while futzing around Windows: the *window control menu.* We see this menu when we click the box in the upper left corner of any window. The Program Manager's control menu looks like figure 5.13. Although not dropping down from the menu bar, this menu behaves like all other menus.

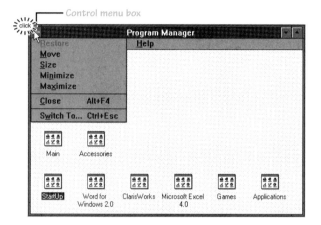

Figure 5.13

The Program Manager's window control menu is similar to the same menu in other windows.

The one command we're interested in here is the next to last one: Close. Fortunately, a double-click of the control menu (or, more precisely, the control box, as it's called) always issues the Close command in all windows and is the most efficient way. Because the Program Manager has special status in Windows, closing it is the same as quitting Windows (the same as the Exit Windows command in its File menu). Don't worry if this sounds confusing. Remember just one thing: double-click the control menu box to close. Do it in the Program Manager to also exit Windows.

A dialog box gives you a chance to stay in Windows (i.e., cancel the Exit command), in case you made the menu choice by accident. All other open applications are shut down (asking you whether you want to store changes you've made to any open documents). At the end, Windows goes away, and you're left at the old DOS C:\> prompt. It is now safe to power down the computer.

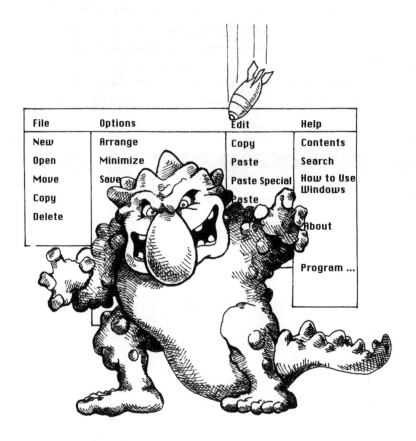

They're Out To Get Us

Because Windows lets us size and position windows all over the place, sometimes the window isn't wide enough to hold all the menus that should be there. When that happens, Windows wraps the menu bar to multiple lines of commands (see fig. 5.14). We access wrapped menus the same way—by clicking on the menu name with the mouse pointer.

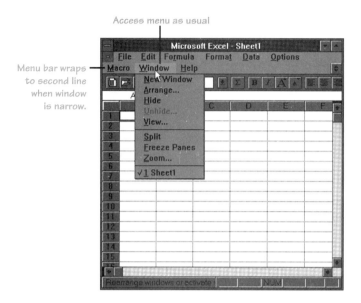

Access menu as usual

Menu bar wraps
to second line
when window
is narrow.

Figure 5.14
*Menu bars can wrap
around when the
window isn't wide
enough to display all
menus.*

Also, if there isn't space on the screen for a menu, Windows looks for the
best fit, even if it means that the menu pops up or off to the side of the
menu name (see fig. 5.15). Don't be alarmed at any of these visual anoma-
lies: they're all normal.

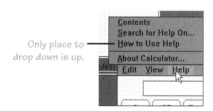

Only place to
drop down is up.

Figure 5.15
*Menus drop down
(or up) wherever
they fit best.*

What happens if you make the wrong menu choice? It happens...regularly.
Fortunately, Windows program designers by and large have anticipated this
possibility. If you've made the wrong choice and something disastrous has
happened, you can usually take everything back by issuing the Undo command in a program's Edit menu shown in figure 5.16. (This command isn't
always available but is in better designed programs.) Furthermore, if the
errant choice leads to a dialog box, click the Cancel button or close the
window (double-clicking the control menu box, mentioned earlier), and
all is put back the way it was.

Practice
Mouse-Menu Action

1. Click on a group icon in the Program Manager window.

2. Pull down the Program Manager's File menu.

3. Slowly drag down the File menu, watching closely how active items highlight as the pointer touches them and how dimmed items don't highlight.

4. Notice dividers between groups of commands and how they don't highlight either.

5. Drag the pointer to the right of the menu and release the mouse button to release the menu without making a selection.

Check Out More Menus

1. Pull down the File menu but don't drag down the menu.

2. Keep the mouse button down and drag the pointer to the Options menu.

3. Continue dragging to the right, watching the Window and Help menus drop down in the process.

Make a Menu Choice

1. Pull down the Help menu.

2. Choose the About Program Manager item as shown in figure 5.17 (it has an ellipsis, so expect a dialog box to appear).

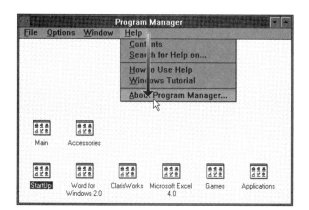

Figure 5.17
*This ellipsis item
leads to a dialog box.*

3. Double-click the control menu box in the dialog box to close the window.

See How Menu Items Can Change

1. Pull down the Options menu and choose Save Settings on Exit.

2. Pull down the Options menu again and notice that if there had been a checkmark to the left of the Save Settings on Exit line, it is gone; if it wasn't there before, it is now. A checkmark means that whatever setting is indicated by the menu item is now engaged (see fig. 5.18).

Checkmark
means that
it's on.

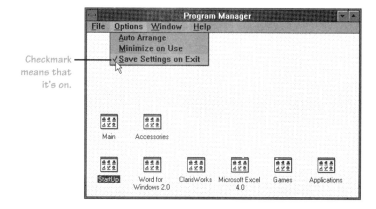

Figure 5.18
*The checkmark
means that the
setting is engaged—
the menu item has
two meanings.*

3. Choose Save Settings on Exit again and look for the status of the checkmark.

Changing from Dimmed to Active

1. Click on any group icon in the Program Manager window.

2. Pull down the File menu and notice that the Move and Copy items are dimmed. Group icons cannot be moved (i.e. to another window), nor can they be copied; thus the menu commands don't apply to a selected group icon.

3. If a group window isn't open, double-click the Main group icon to open its window (see fig. 5.19).

Figure 5.19
Double-click the
Main group icon.

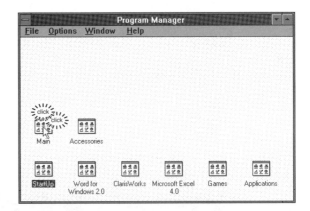

4. Click on any program item in the group window.

5. Pull down the File menu and see that both Move and Copy are now active, because program item icons can be moved (from one group to another) or duplicated.

Keyboard Equivalents

1. Click anywhere in the Main window.

2. Click once on the Control menu at the upper left corner of the Main window. Notice the keyboard equivalent for the Close command, Ctrl+F4.

3. Click outside the menu to close it.

4. Hold down the Control key and press the F4 key. The window closes.

5. Momentarily hold down the Program Manager's File menu and notice that the Enter key is the keyboard equivalent of the Open command.

6. Click the Main group icon and then press Enter. The Main window re-opens.

Exiting Windows

1. Double-click the control menu box in the Program Manager's window (see fig. 5.20).

Figure 5.20

Double-clicking the control menu box closes the window—and in the case of the Program Manager, Windows, too.

2. In response to the dialog box, click the OK button. You return to the DOS prompt or shell.

3. You can now turn off your PC unless you're going on to the next encounter.

Summary

Menus are the primary way we tell Windows what to do next. Even if we don't have a clue about what the next step may be in operating a program, pulling down the menus may jog our memories about what to do. Commands that all programs have in common are always in the same menu and go by the same name (or close enough); most of these commands can also be initiated by typing a keyboard equivalent. Finally, the safe way to leave Windows before shutting off your PC is by closing the Program Manager's window.

Exorcises

1. What do three periods after a menu item mean?

2. How can you make a dimmed menu item become active?

3. What is the most mouse-efficient way to close a window?

4. Why should you exit Windows via the Program Manager instead of simply switching off the computer?

Window with a View

Goal

Learn how to manage on-screen windows most
efficiently.

What You Will Need

PC turned on with Windows running.

Terms of Enfearment

title bar	minimize button
active window	maximize button
inactive window	restore button
window border	control menu box
window corner	

Briefing

We've seen some windows previously, but now it's time to examine more closely the things that give Windows its name—the on-screen windows. Windows likes to give us lots of flexibility in the way we do things on the screen, and its on-screen windows are no exception. Even better, what we learn about desktop windows (like the Program Manager) applies to most other windows.

Entitlebarment

Windows contain several controls that let us determine how things look and where they are on the screen. For instance, across the top of every window is a *title bar* (see fig. 6.1). The title bar displays the name of the program that owns that window. Color (or black on a monochrome screen) that fills the title bar also tells a story: the window filled with a color and whose title is in white is called the *active window* (see fig. 6.2). This is the window—among however many layers of windows that may be on the screen—that is on top of the pile, just like the item that's on top of the heap of stuff strewn around your physical desk. Only one window can be active at a time. An *inactive window's* title bar is usually white with black type (but may be slightly different in some color schemes). To make any window the active window, all it takes is a click of the pointer anywhere on that window, even if only on the slightest sliver hanging out from beneath another window on the screen.

Figure 6.1
Window title bar.

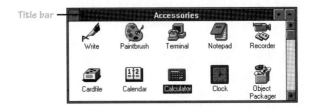

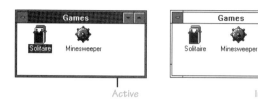

Figure 6.2
Inactive window (left) and active window (right). Active window title bars are usually colored or black.

The title bar is also the means by which we move windows around the screen. Click and drag in the title bar. As we drag the window, we drag just its outline. Position the outline where we want it, release the mouse button, and the actual window zips to that spot (see fig. 6.3).

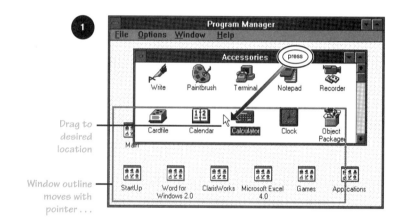

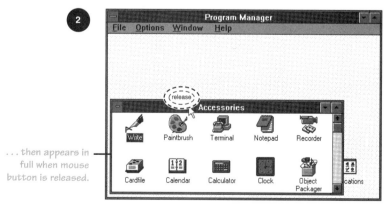

Figure 6.3
To move a window, drag its title bar.

Drag to desired location

Window outline moves with pointer . . .

. . . then appears in full when mouse button is released.

Resizing Windows

We can also resize a window from any direction. All edges and corners of a window can be stretched as you like.

As you slowly roll the pointer atop a *window border*, the pointer shape changes from a single diagonal arrow to a two-headed arrow (see fig. 6.4). This bi-directional arrow indicates in what directions we can click and drag that border. At each of the four *window corners* are subtle corner indicators. Roll the pointer atop one of those, and the pointer changes to a diagonal two-headed arrow, meaning that we can drag virtually in any direction.

Figure 6.4
The pointer changes to a two-headed arrow when rolled atop a window border or a window corner (1). Drag either to resize the window as desired (2).

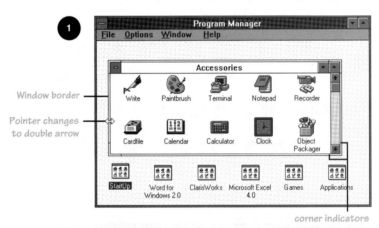

Window border

Pointer changes to double arrow

corner indicators

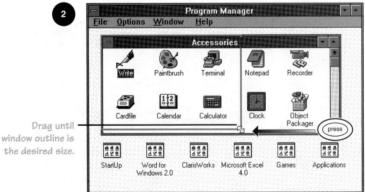

Drag until window outline is the desired size.

While we're on the subject of resizing a window, notice the two arrow buttons at the right edge of the title bar. Each one performs a very different function.

Press-To Change-O

The down arrow is called the *minimize button.* In Windows-speak, minimizing means that the window shrinks to an icon at the bottom of the Windows desktop (see fig. 6.5). The program is still running (and any open document that may a part of that program is also still open, but just shrunken). A double-click of the icon opens the window back up—it *restores* the window.

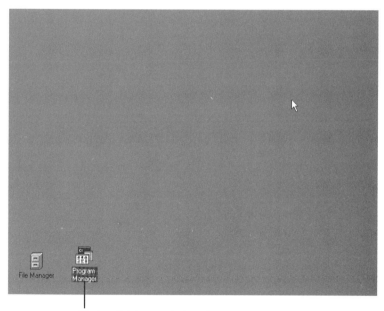

Figure 6.5
The minimize button shrinks the window to a desktop icon. Double-clicking the icon restores the window to its previous size.

Window shrinks to a desktop icon.

The up arrow is called the *maximize button.* As you might guess, this instructs the window to occupy the entire screen, hiding everything else that might be open or visible on the desktop (see fig. 6.6). After you maximize a window, a funny thing happens to the button: it changes to a two-headed arrow. Its formal name has changed, too—the *restore button*. All this means is that a click restores the window to its previous size and location on the desktop.

Figure 6.6

Click the maximize button to make the window fill the screen. Click the restore button to make the window draggable and resizable.

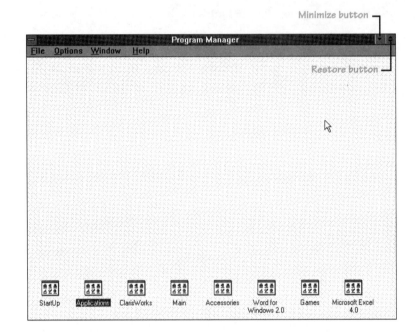

Closing Windows

At the left edge of the title bar is a button that is unnecessarily complex for mouse-using Windows folks, like us. A click of this *control menu box* reveals a number of options that affect the active window. The good news is that because all these menu items are here for keyboard-only users of Windows, we can ignore every item there. What we use this control menu button for is to close the window with a double-click (the same as choosing Close in the menu).

A Vast Vista

Quite often, the amount of stuff in a window is greater than the screen space available for it. Here's where we get to see that a window is really just a view to what may be a larger space. To see the rest of the items, we don't reposition the window, but the space beneath it (see fig. 6.7). It's like working with a microfilm or microfiche reader: we view the contents through a fixed lens and move the film to bring the desired contents into view.

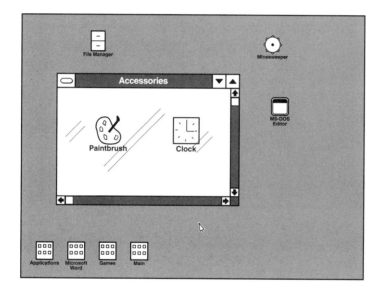

Figure 6.7
Scroll bars let us adjust our view to a larger space than shows through the window.

Our controls for moving the window's contents are called *scroll bars* (see fig. 6.8). Scroll bars appear along the right and/or bottom edges of windows only when the information is larger than the current window size.

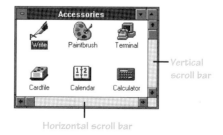

Figure 6.8
Scroll bars appear in windows whenever the window isn't big enough to display all its contents.

Scroll Bar Pieces

A live scroll bar has four elements to help navigate in either the vertical or horizontal direction (see fig. 6.9). At each edge of a scroll bar are scroll arrow buttons. A click of the button scrolls the window's view of the contents in that direction by one unit (this unit varies with the type of information being viewed in the window). Note the distinction—we scroll in the direction of our view to the contents, not the direction that the contents move.

Figure 6.9

A scroll bar consists of five controls we click or drag to adjust our view.

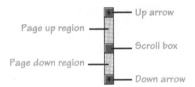

As we scroll in any direction, the square indicator shows the position of the current view in relation to the available space (the gray pattern area of the scroll bar). It's like an electronic version of knowing how far we are in a book, in which we can see the bulk of pages we've passed compared to the chunk yet to go. Clicking and holding down a scroll arrow puts scrolling in rapid-fire action.

To jump to some approximate spot, we can click and drag this indicator (called the *scroll box*, a forgettable term) to about where we want to go (see fig. 6.10). In some windows, the view changes as we drag the scroll box, so we can quickly get where we need.

Figure 6.10

We can drag the scroll box to any spot along the scroll bar to jump ahead or back.

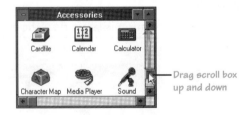

One other scrolling increment at our disposal—clicking in the gray area on either side of the scroll box—shifts our view in screenful chunks. These clickable areas usually mimic presses of the PgUp and PgDn keyboard keys.

They're Out To Get Us

Because it is easy to activate an underlying window by clicking on it, the strong possibility exists that a newly activated window will completely obscure a smaller window that had previously been on top (see fig. 6.11). The small window isn't gone. In fact, unless you specifically close it, the window will always be there. To access this obscured window on the desktop, you can either move or resize other windows until you can see any part of the smaller window to click on or look for a Window menu, from which you can choose any window from the list of available windows (see fig. 6.12).

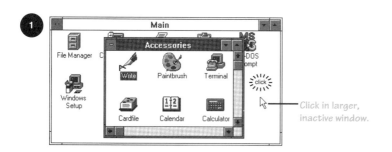

Figure 6.11
A click on a larger, underlying window can completely hide the smaller window.

Figure 6.11
continued

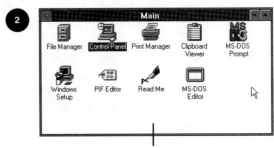

Large, active window covers smaller window.

Figure 6.12
*A Window menu
can help you re-
activate the smaller
window.*

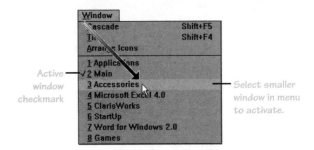

Active
window
checkmark

Select smaller
window in menu
to activate.

As you work with Windows, you may encounter other window styles, some
of which are standard Windows material, and others designed by programmers to mimic window styles from other computer systems. Don't be
alarmed if you should see window styles that lack one or more of the following: scroll bars, minimize button, or maximize button. Moreover, the title
bar may look quite different. When a control is missing, it usually means
that the window's behavior is narrower than typical windows.

Practice
Window Calisthenics

1. Drag the Program Manager window around the screen by its title bar;
   release the mouse button. Do this several times to get the feel of
   dragging the window outline. Leave the window in a position so that
   all four corners are visible.

2. Place the pointer atop one straight edge of the window border until the pointer turns into the two-headed arrow.

3. Drag the edge of the window in each direction, releasing the mouse button after each drag.

4. Drag a window corner and resize the window a couple of times. See how small you can resize the window. Notice two important events:

   a. What happens to the menu bar when the window isn't wide enough to display all menus in one line.

   b. What happens in the scroll bar when the window is sized smaller than space containing icons.

5. Finally, resize the window to an intermediate size so that no scroll bars appear.

To the Max and Min

1. Click the maximize button (upper right corner) to see how Windows sizes the window to its full-screen size. Also notice that the button has turned into a restore button.

2. Click the restore button to restore the window to its previous size.

3. Click the minimize button. The Program Manager window shrinks to an icon in the desktop.

4. Double-click the icon to restore the Program Manager window to its previous size.

Scrolling

1. Arrange the Program Manager group icons so that they are in columns of at least three icons tall.

2. Resize the Program Manager window to cause scroll bars to appear.

3. Drag the scroll box up and down the scroll bar, watching the contents move along with it. Then drag the scroll box to the top and release.

4. Resize the Program Manager to its approximate original size and choose Arrange Icons from the Window menu.

Summary

We've learned much more about how to control a window. No matter how many windows are open on the desktop, only one—the active window—is on top of the pile. Window controls found in windows—for moving, resizing, maximizing, minimizing, scrolling, and closing—are the same controls you'll find in other windows throughout your Windows work.

Exorcises

1. Match the window components' names to the blanks on the illustration in figure 6.13.

   a. title bar

   b. control menu

   c. window border

   d. maximize button

   e. minimize button

   f. horizontal scroll bar

   g. vertical scroll bar

   h. window name

2. Describe what happens when you click on or drag the following window controls: window corner; scroll down arrow; page down area; title bar; minimize button.

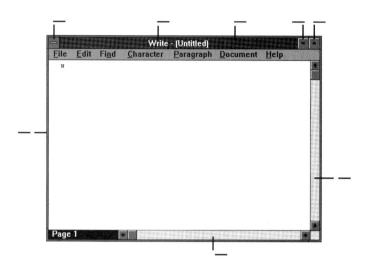

Figure 6.13
*Match the
components.*

What's in Your Machine

Goal

Learn how to use the File Manager to show you everything you need to know about your PC and its contents.

What You Will Need

PC turned on with Windows running.

Terms of Enfearment

folder	root
File Manager	megabyte
drive	kilobyte
directory	directory window
subdirectory	tree
file name	memory
extension	RAM
path	virtual memory

Briefing
A Giant Filing Cabinet

Earlier, we introduced the idea that the hard disk in your PC is like a giant filing cabinet. It contains documents, programs, and *folders*; those folders, in turn, can hold additional documents, programs, and other folders. The hard disk also contains a bunch of stuff that the PC needs to behave like a PC—most of it is in a folder named DOS.

Without a doubt, the most important program that comes with Windows is the *File Manager* (see fig. 7.1). This program lets us peer into the vastness of our hard disk and then organize its contents so that it all makes sense to our programs and us. The File Manager doesn't start up automatically when you begin Windows (although we'll see how to make it happen later), unless someone has modified the copy of Windows running on your PC.

Figure 7.1

The File Manager window.

To start up the File Manager, you must find its icon in the Program Manager. Windows installs the File Manager icon in the Main group. Open the Main group and double-click the File Manager icon to start it up. Despite all the pretty parts about using Windows productively, working with the hard disk reminds us that Windows sits on top of MS-DOS and must use DOS's disk filing facilities. Therefore, to understand what's going on in the File Manager window requires a brief side trip to learn a few DOS basics.

Fear DOS No More (Windows Edition)

Lesson number one about DOS (and 50 percent of what you need to know) is how to pronounce it. DOS rhymes with boss, not dose.

Easy As A, B, C...

Disk volumes in DOS—called *drives*—are signified by letters. Drives A and B are reserved for floppy disk drives. Your PC probably has an internal floppy disk drive, set up as drive A. Most hard disks, therefore, are set up with the next available letter, C (it doesn't have to be C, but usually is). If additional disks or other kinds of volumes (such as a disk drive from another computer available to you via a network) are connected to your PC, they'll each have a unique letter.

Folder = Directory

We spoke earlier about folders in the hard disk "filing cabinet." Although the File Manager displays these items as folders, DOS calls these groupings *directories* (see fig. 7.2). Because one folder may contain files plus other folders, a directory may contain files plus one or more other directories. You can spot old-old-timers in DOS when they use the term *subdirectory* when referring to nested directories.

Selected drive   Directory name corresponds to selected folder

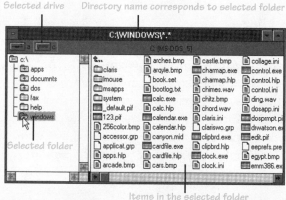

Selected folder

Items in the selected folder

Figure 7.2

A File Manager folder is also called a directory, which can contain files and other directories.

The Name Game

Every item—directory or file—on a hard disk has a name. DOS imposes a limit to the length of names we can assign to directories and files: 11 characters, divided into two parts of 8 and 3 characters each—separated by a period. On top of that are all kinds of rules about things to avoid in file names.

To simplify, here are directory and file-naming guidelines that should be easier to remember:

- Limit directory names to 8 characters.

- Limit document file names to 8 characters and let the program you're using worry about the last three (after the period).

- Use only letters and numbers for item names (avoid punctuation marks).

- Use one-word names only, even if it means concocting the most bizarre abbreviations to make your "1993 Budget Forecast Model" spreadsheet file fit in an 8-character name (BFcstM93).

The last three characters after the period in a file name are called a file *extension*. Most programs generate files with an extension (hopefully) unique to that program. For example, Microsoft Excel appends the extension xls after each spreadsheet file it stores on the disk. Extensions will come in handy later.

Pathway to the Files

The last part of DOS to get in your face while in Windows is the concept of the pathname. A *path* is a roadmap to any file (see fig. 7.3). It assumes that you start the trip not knowing anything, including which disk drive the file lives in. Therefore, the path provides the disk drive letter and the name of each directory you need to "open" your way to the file. Each element of this pathname is separated by a weird backslash character (\). The following are some path examples and what they mean:

Path: `C:\autoexec.bat`

Means: A file named autoexec (with an extension bat) is at the very first level of stuff on the C drive. This level is called the *root* level.

Path: `C:\apps\123.exe`

Means: A file named 123 (with an extension of exe) is in a directory called Apps on the C drive.

Path: `C:\windows\system\vgalogo.lgo`

Means: A file named vgalogo (with an extension of lgo) is in a directory called system, inside a directory called windows on the C drive.

Path: `C:\documnts\fearwnot\text\encntr07.doc`

Means: A file named encntr07 (with an extension doc) is inside a directory called text, inside a directory called Fearwnot, inside a directory called Documnts on the C drive.

Folder path in icon form   Folder path in text form

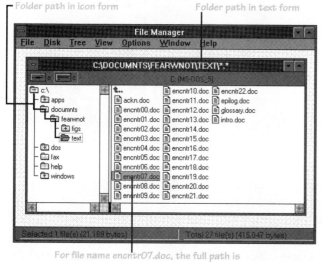

Figure 7.3

How Windows views the paths as items in nested folders.

For file name encntr07.doc, the full path is
c:\documnts\fearwnot\text\encntr07.doc

Half Full or Half Empty?

As you work with Windows, it is important to keep an eye on how much empty space there is in the hard disk so that you can store new documents. Hard disks are measured in a unit called the *megabyte* (one megabyte is equivalent to approximately one million typed characters). The File Manager, however, gets more detailed about our disk's size by telling us in *kilobytes* (approximately one thousand characters). We can see at a glance at the bottom of the File Manager window how many kilobytes (KBs) of our hard disk are occupied and how many are available for additional stuff (see fig. 7.4). As items are added or deleted, the File Manager keeps these figures up to date for us.

Figure 7.4

The File Manager shows us the current status of the selected drive.

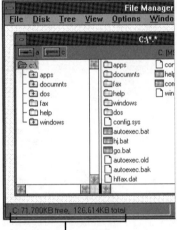

Status of selected drive

Window in a Window

What may not be apparent the first time you start up the File Manager is that most of the action takes place in a second window that floats around inside the File Manager window. Below the menu bar is the title bar of a window that lets us view and manipulate the contents of any selected disk drive. The official name for this window is a *directory window*. We can open multiple directory windows within the File Manager as shown in figure 7.5 (indeed, this multiple window idea within a program comes in handy when working with documents, as we'll see later), but we'll leave that for more advanced filing tasks.

Directory window for drive A

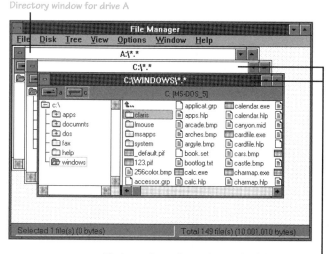

Figure 7.5

We can view directory windows for more than one directory at a time— either from different parts of the same drive or from multiple drives.

Windows of two directories on the C drive—one is the root; the other is the Windows Folder.

Directory Window Panes

More obvious is the fact that a directory window is divided into two panes (resizable by dragging the dividing bar left or right). On the left is a graphical view of the folder structure of the selected drive—the directory *tree* (see fig. 7.6). Double-clicking on a folder in the tree reveals further folders (if any) nested inside (see fig.7.7). As we click (or double-click) any folder in the tree, we immediately see the contents of that folder in the right pane.

Figure 7.6
A directory window's parts.

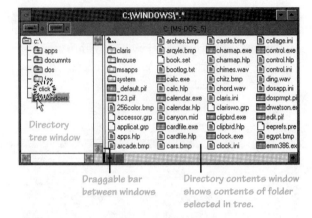

Draggable bar
between windows

Directory contents window
shows contents of folder
selected in tree.

Figure 7.7
Click a folder in the tree to see the contents at the right. Double-click any folder to expand (or collapse) the branch nested inside.

Double-click to see
nested folders in
tree.

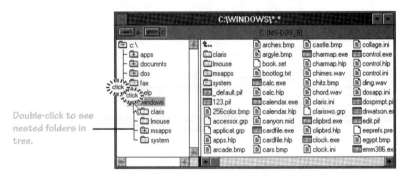

Icons in the contents pane of the directory window tell us a lot about each file:

Icon	Description
	A directory inside the currently selected directory
	A program icon
	A document file generated by a program you use
	Any other file, including documents not associated with any program

As you click on any file in the right contents pane, its size (in bytes) appears in the lower left message area of that window. Folders, confusingly, show themselves to be zero bytes in size, when, in fact, they may contain many files.

Filing Cabinet Folders

The folder icons in the File Manager help us organize the information on our hard disks. Just like the paper folders of the old-fashioned office (like the ones we all work in), folders allow us to collect related stuff, label the folder by name, and carry everything in the folder as one convenient item. Windows folders, however, aren't very limited in how many things they can hold. In fact, they can even hold other folders, which can hold other folders, and so on, until you've probably lost what it is you were trying to organize.

Although the root level of your particular PC's hard disk may have lots of folders in them, two are very important: DOS and WINDOWS. The DOS folder contains almost everything that your PC needs to start up as an MS-DOS machine (a prerequisite for being a Windows machine). The WINDOWS folder contains everything your PC needs to become a Windows machine. You rarely need to go inside these folders, except when a program you acquire automatically installs itself into one of these folders, and you need to move the program to a more logical place.

Generic versus Pretty Icons

It's important to notice that program and document icons in the File Manager are generic: all program files have the same icon, for example. It's only in the Program Manager that we get to see colorful, distinctive icons for programs and their documents. While the File Manager is showing us real files—one icon per item—the Program Manager presents an artificial dashboard for us to organize and access representations of items—multiple copies of an item, if we like—in a simpler visual environment.

Some users prefer to use only the File Manager (double-clicking program files to start applications); still others supplement Windows with software from outside sources, such as the Norton Desktop for Windows shown in

figure 7.8 (Symantec Corp.), which combines the many functions and
features of the File Manager and Program Manager into one desktop screen.
These are all acceptable ways to use Windows, but for the purposes of this
book, we'll continue to address using both File Manager and Program
Manager.

Figure 7.8

*The Norton Desktop
for Windows
combines aspects of
the File and
Program Manager
functions on the
desktop.*

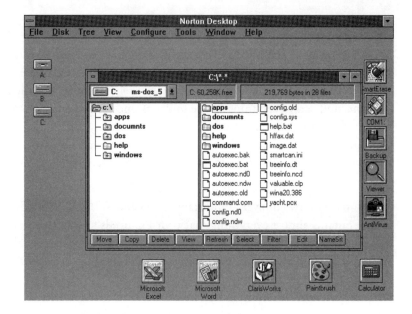

Short-Term Memory

Another critical measurement of your PC's capabilities in Windows is
something called *memory* (also, interchangeably, *RAM* for random access
memory). Memory is measured both in terms of kilobytes, or thousands of
characters, represented by the letter K and megabytes (M, MB, or Megs).

When discussing the amount of RAM inside a PC, the megabyte number is
the one to use. The value is generally a number ranging from two to tens of
megabytes. The maximum amount of RAM a PC may hold depends entirely
on the PC model you have; the minimum recommended for productive
work in Windows is four megabytes.

Memory Check

Although Windows doesn't let you know how much memory is installed in your PC, it does provide a readout of how much RAM is available at any moment. The problem is that it may show your machine to have far more memory available to Windows than there are physical RAM chips on your PC. The reason is that when possible (for example, if your PC has the horsepower and available disk space), Windows automatically sets up a part of your hard disk to act as additional RAM (*virtual memory*, it's called) when Windows needs more RAM than you have installed. Although this sounds neat, access to this part of memory is much slower than real chip RAM, and you'll see your hard disk light blinking a lot.

To check how much total memory (chip and virtual RAM) is available to Windows, choose the About item in almost any program's Help menu. Somewhere in the dialog box that appears will be a description of the amount of memory remaining free (see fig. 7.9). The memory value is related in kilobytes (K).

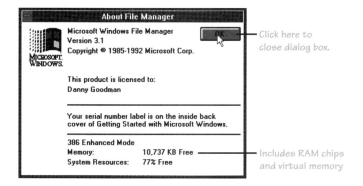

Figure 7.9

Choose About in any Help menu to see how much memory (real and virtual) is available.

To correlate this value to a megabyte rating, divide the K number by 1,024 (I don't have the time to explain, and you probably don't have the patience to learn, how a computer considers a thousand of anything to actually be 1,024). For example, a total memory of 8,192K evaluates to 8 megabytes.

Two Different Animals

Despite the confusion caused by virtual memory, RAM is very different from disk storage. RAM is temporary. The instant you shut down your PC, contents of RAM are forgotten history (even virtual memory on the disk is wiped out). RAM is like a chalkboard in a classroom. To work on a problem for the class, the teacher copies a problem from the lesson plan onto the board. While working on the problem, all action is on the blackboard. Because the board will be washed clean at night, it is vital that the work in progress be copied down on paper and stored away (in a filing cabinet) so that it can be retrieved tomorrow. That's why our machines have hard disks that act like filing cabinets: to preserve great amounts of information from session to session.

They're Out To Get Us

Sometimes a hard disk can fill up. When this happens, you could be in trouble if you need to save changes to a big document. There are ways to get out of the jam, but the best solution is to avoid getting too full in the first place. I'll have some recommendations about that in the 20th Encounter

It seems we're almost invited to click on the icons for the floppy drive(s) in a File Manager window. But, if there is no diskette in a drive when you click, an error message appears (see fig. 7.10). The message dialog box gives you a chance to insert a disk and retry access or to just cancel the box and go on about your business.

Figure 7.10
*Click a floppy drive
icon in the File
Manager, and this is
what you see if the
drive lacks a diskette.*

Without a doubt, the most confusing part of PCs, RAM, and Windows is knowing how your PC is configured, especially if your PC is an older model. It's not just a case of knowing how many megabytes of RAM are installed. Windows tries its best to set up your PC's RAM for optimum Windows performance, but add-in memory boards may be configured so that Windows can't take advantage of it. This is not the place for beginners. Find a dealer or experienced PC freak to help you out. When things are set up properly, no further adjustments should be necessary.

Practice
Check the Hard Disk

1. Start Windows as you learned in the 2nd Encounter.

2. From the Program Manager window, double-click the Main group icon to open its window.

3. Double-click the File Manager icon.

4. Look for the amount of free space on your hard disk at the bottom of the window.

Quick Tour of Your Disk

1. Double-click the C:\ folder at the top of the tree in the left pane of the File Manager window. This closes up the entire tree.

2. Double-click the C:\ folder again to view the first level of folders (the root) on the C drive.

3. Click on each of the folders in the tree diagram on the left side of the File Manager window. Notice the files and folders in each as displayed in the right pane.

4. Double-click the Windows folder in the tree. Notice that some additional folders are nested in the Windows folder. Click on each of those to see what files they contain.

Check the Memory

1. Choose About File Manager from the Help Menu. The About File Manager dialog box appears (see fig. 7.9).

2. Divide the number of kilobytes in the Total Memory listing by 1,024.

3. Double-click the control menu icon in the upper left corner of the window to close the window.

Summary

The hard disk is the long-term storage area for documents and programs. Items can be organized into folders (directories), which may be nested inside other folders, and we use the File Manager to organize all this stuff. Disk space is measured in kilobytes (KB), and items on the disk are usually measured in bytes. It takes 1,024 bytes to make one kilobyte. RAM is a temporary storage area where actual work is done on documents by programs. RAM contents are erased when the machine shuts down, so all work is saved to the hard disk.

Exorcises

1. If you write and store 10 business letters a day and if each letter occupies 4KB (roughly 4000 characters) of disk space, how many days will it take you to fill up one megabyte of disk space?

2. Match the icons in figure 7.11 to their descriptions:

   a. drive

   b. document

   c. program

   d. directory

3. Describe the differences between program icons in the File Manager and program icons in the Program Manager.

Figure 7.11
Match the icons to their descriptions.

Getting Organized— Files

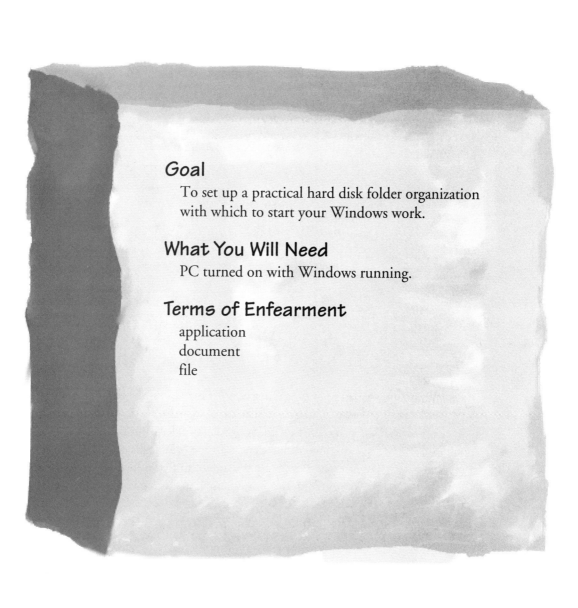

Goal

To set up a practical hard disk folder organization with which to start your Windows work.

What You Will Need

PC turned on with Windows running.

Terms of Enfearment

application
document
file

Briefing

Folders Full of Files

As you'll see later, the work we really do with Windows is inside *application* programs—things like word processors, spreadsheets, databases, and the like. All of these programs generate *documents*, which we store on the hard disk (see fig. 8.1). Each document, as well as each program, resides on the hard disk as a *file*. This is an old computing term that dates back to before many of us were born.

Figure 8.1

A Program Manager group for ClarisWorks (a Windows program) displays different icons for the program (its documents).

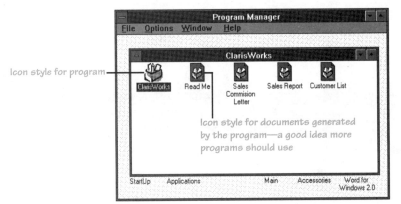

Real World versus Computer Files

In a filing cabinet metaphor, your idea of a file may be confused by the typical practice to casually refer to a file as a folder of stuff. If you were ever hauled down to the principal's office, your file (a folder from the filing cabinet) would have been front-and-center on the principal's desk. In computerdom, however, each separate document in that folder (your attendance record, your grades, the forged absentee excuse) is considered a file.

Essentially, a file is a separate entity on the hard disk that has a name and other attributes that differentiate it from other files. A program like

Microsoft Word, for example, is a file unto itself, but it also relies on other files that give the program powers to check the spelling of our documents, to remember program settings we've made, and to perform automatic hyphenation. Each document (e.g., letter, memo, newsletter article) we create and name is also a separate file that resides on the hard disk (see fig. 8.2).

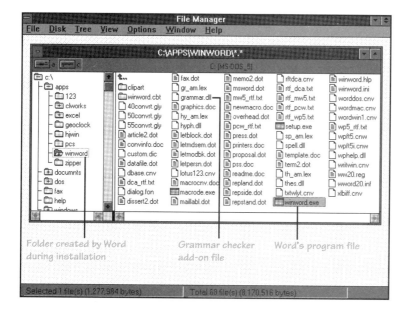

Figure 8.2
This Word for Windows directory window shows all the files installed with the program. Only one file, winword.exe, is the actual program.

The bottom line? Any icon we see in the File Manager listing—except folders—is a file. Period.

Why Organize?

Organizing these files on your hard disk is an important maintenance task. It's like checking the oil periodically on your car: you can ignore it for a while, but if you let it go forever, you're likely to get into trouble of some kind.

Because your hard disk may eventually contain thousands of files, it is important to establish a method to the madness. How you organize the files depends a lot on your view of your computing world. Two of the most common ways of grouping items are by application and by subject.

One (Old-Fashioned) Method

Organizing a hard disk by application is more computer oriented. Such an organization is shown in figure 8.3. At the root level are folders for each application. The implication is that documents for each application are stored inside those folders as well (perhaps inside other folders).

Figure 8.3
Organization by application makes us think too much in computer terms ("What program created the document I need?").

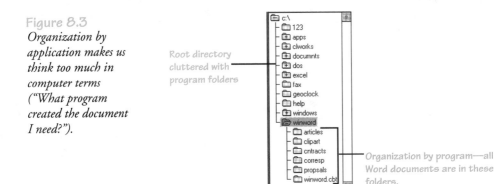

Root directory cluttered with program folders

Organization by program—all Word documents are in these folders.

New Fashioned, but Just as Bad

When you run through the installation processes of many Windows-based applications, they recommend that you place their folders inside the Windows folder (see fig. 8.4). For example, you could have Microsoft Word, Excel, and FileMaker Pro folders inside your Windows folder. Believe me, the Windows folder is crowded enough without adding applications folders. It also could make upgrading Windows more difficult for you in the future.

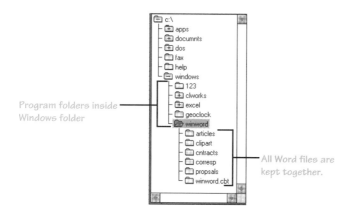

Program folders inside Windows folder

All Word files are kept together.

Figure 8.4
Throwing all Windows-based applications into the Windows folder still focuses your attention too much on the computer.

One (Recommended) Method

Organizing the disk by subject is more like the way you organize a filing cabinet and is the way I recommend. Figure 8.5 shows a typical way to start such an organization at the root level. It groups all application programs into one folder, called Apps. There tend to be so many files that comprise each program (see fig. 8.2 as one example), that it's best to keep each program's folder as is within the Apps folder. There may be identically named files from each program, which prevent the programs from being at the same level.

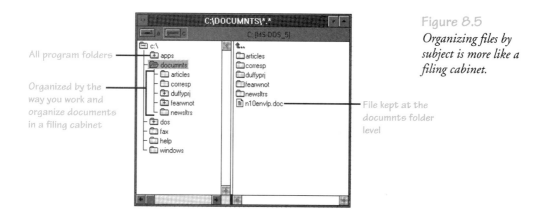

All program folders

Organized by the way you work and organize documents in a filing cabinet

File kept at the documnts folder level

Figure 8.5
Organizing files by subject is more like a filing cabinet.

Another folder, called Documnts, is where you will store all files that you create. Inside will be additional folders, named for their subject—along the same lines as you would categorize, group, and file them in a filing cabinet (see fig. 8.6). Examples would be folders for all correspondence for a given month, a folder for a project, a folder for a customer, and a folder for all financial information.

Figure 8.6

We easily can combine documents from different applications in a subject folder. Here, we have all relevant files for the Duffy project in one folder.

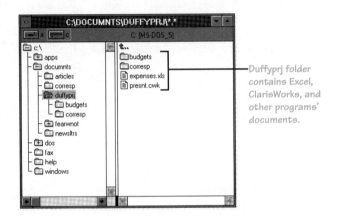

Why It's Better

The reason this method makes more sense than the by-application method is that we are now free to use whatever combination of programs we want to generate documents for the given subject. For example, a folder for a specific project may contain a spreadsheet of the budget, several word processing documents for proposals and correspondence, electronic mail messages between the participants, electronic drawings, project schedules, and so on. You think of these things according to their context within your work life—not by the program that created each document.

New Folders

Using the File Manager to create directories is easy. In the directory tree, click once on the folder *into which* you want the new folder to go. Then choose Create Directory from the File menu. A dialog box appears, with a field for us to enter a name (see fig. 8.7). Remember to limit the name to eight characters and that the name can't be a duplicate of another folder at the same level. Windows automatically converts the name we type to lowercase, so don't bother typing capital letters.

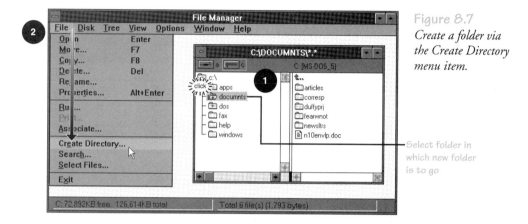

Figure 8.7
Create a folder via the Create Directory menu item.

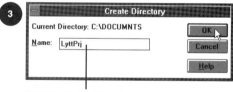

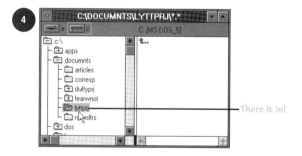

Changing a Folder Name

After a folder is named, we can rename it at any time. Click once on the folder to select it. Then choose Rename from the File menu. A dialog box appears, showing the old name and providing a field for entering the new name (see fig. 8.8). Click the OK button for the change to take effect. This technique for renaming folders also applies to renaming files.

Figure 8.8

Rename a folder (or file) via the Rename dialog box.

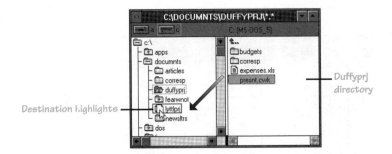

Moving Items Around

Moving a file or folder from one location to another is as simple as dragging the item from either side of a File Manager directory window to the desired location and dropping it onto the folder in which it should go (see fig. 8.9). As you drag something, you can drag it only to an item that highlights (with a rectangle around it). This graphically reinforces where you're about to drop an item.

Figure 8.9

Moving an item from one folder to another.

The trickiest part of moving an item, however, is that you need to see both the item you're dragging and the destination folder in one view.

The most efficient way to handle this is to always drag an item from the right pane (even if it is a folder) to a folder in the left pane as shown in figure 8.10 (although nothing prevents you from dragging and dropping all within a single pane). It may take a bit of coordination to get the following steps down:

1. Expand the tree view so that you see the destination folder.

2. Select the folder containing the item you want to move. A listing of that folder's contents appears in the right pane.

3. If necessary, scroll the tree pane again so that you see the destination folder.

4. Click and drag that item to the destination folder in the tree.

Until the tree gets very big, remember that we can maximize the File Manager window, which shows quite a bit more of the tree without scrolling.

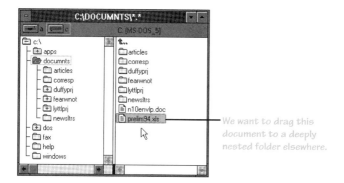

We want to drag this document to a deeply nested folder elsewhere.

Figure 8.10

A complex move involving deeply nested folders requires expanding the tree view before selecting the folder containing the item to be moved.

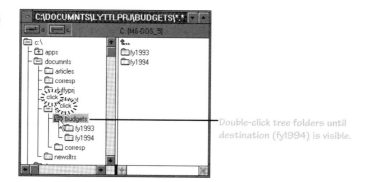

Double-click tree folders until destination (fy1994) is visible.

Figure 8.10
continued

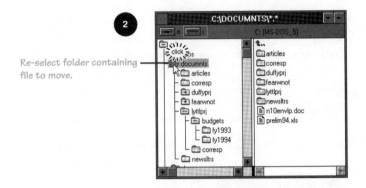

Re-select folder containing file to move.

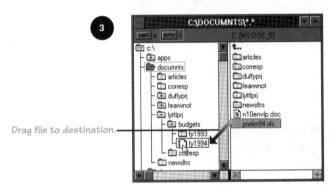

Drag file to destination.

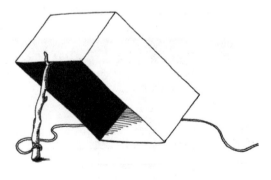

They're Out To Get Us

To help itself keep things straight, DOS/Windows doesn't allow two items to have the same name at the same folder level. A hard disk may contain 20 files and folders named "Joe Blow," but no more than one can be at the same folder level. If you try to drag an item to a folder containing another item by the same name, Windows alerts you to the fact as shown in figure 8.11 and puts things back the way they were before you dragged.

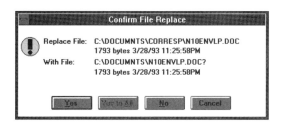

Figure 8.11

Trying to drag an item to a destination already containing an item by that name.

You don't have to be a neatness freak to realize that a hard disk can get unruly in a hurry. Try to keep it clean. Also, it will be helpful if you keep the root level relatively clutter-free. It's OK to bring a folder you're using a lot to the root but put it back when access requirements diminish.

Some Windows experts follow self-imposed guidelines about how many items should be at any given level. You can develop your own scheme as you get used to the system; you are in charge. You'll learn in the 10th Encounter how to search a hard disk for anything in case you forget where a file is.

If there is one teeth-gritting frustration in working with files and folders, it's having things happen—creating a folder or moving a file into a folder—in the wrong folder level. This is apt to happen while moving things around the File Manager, even when it constantly asks for confirmation before such moves. Fortunately, nothing we do (short of erasing a file or folder as discussed in the 9th Encounter) is irreparable, because we can keep dragging things around until they're where we want them.

Practice

Creating and Naming Folders

1. In the File Manager directory tree, select the C:\ folder.

2. Choose Create Directory from the File menu (see fig. 8.12). A dialog box appears requesting a directory name.

3. Type folder1 and press Return to create the folder.

Figure 8.12

Naming a new directory.

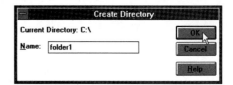

4. Choose Create Directory again.

5. Try assigning the same name—*folder1* to the new folder. Notice the warning that the name is already taken (at least for inside this window).

6. Click folder1 to select it.

7. Choose Create Directory once more and assign the name folder1. Windows accepts this, because there is only one item in that directory by the name *folder1*.

8. Select the new, nested folder1 icon.

9. Choose Rename from the File menu.

10. Assign the name folder2 to this folder.

11. Select folder1 again, create another folder here, and name it *folder3* (see fig. 8.13).

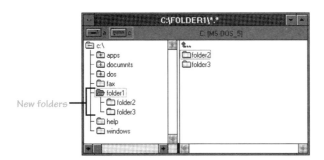

Figure 8.13
*Three new folders as
they should look in
the directory tree.*

Moving a Folder of Stuff

1. Drag folder1 to the Windows folder. Everything inside that folder
   came along with it.

2. Double-click the Windows folder once or twice (as needed) until all
   folders inside the Windows folder appear on the tree diagram. Figure
   8.14 shows that folder1 is now one of the folders in the Windows
   folder.

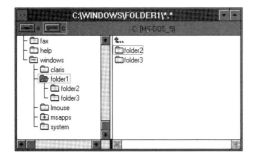

Figure 8.14
*The Windows folder
now contains folder1
and its contents.*

Moving Multiple Items

1. Drag the folder2 icon to the Windows folder icon, placing folder2 at
   the same level as folder1. Do the same for folder3. We cannot select
   more than one item at a time from the tree diagram.

2. Select the Windows folder icon. The Windows folder contents (folders and files) appear in the right pane.

3. We're going to drag the three new folders to the C:\ folder icon in the directory tree, so scroll the tree diagram, if necessary, until the C:\ folder is visible.

4. Hold down the Control key and click on each of the three new folders in the right pane. Each one stays selected (see fig. 8.15).

Figure 8.15
Control-clicking items in the contents pane allows for multiple item selections.

Hold down the Ctrl key and click on each file.

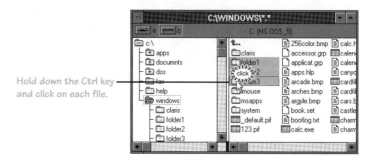

5. Release the Control key and place the pointer on any one of the selected folders. Drag the folder to the C:\ folder icon (see fig. 8.16). All three folders go into the root level.

Figure 8.16
Dragging all selected items to the C:\ folder.

All selected items moved with one drag motion

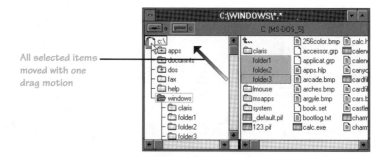

6. Select the C:\ folder. All items in the root, including the three new folders, appear in the right pane.

7. Control-select the three new folders in the right pane.

8. Choose Delete from the File menu and confirm that you want to delete these items. We'll discuss more about deleting items in the next chapter.

Setting Up Your Folders

1. Unless you've been instructed by someone to follow another organization method, begin by making sure that your hard disk root directory contains at least these four folders: DOS (or MS-DOS), WINDOWS, Apps, and Documnts. The setup routine for your PC may place other folders, such as Help, at the root level, where they should stay.

2. Locate folders you can identify as containing programs. Their names may be explicit or cryptic, depending on how long their trade names are. For example, Lotus 1-2-3's folder is called 123; Microsoft Word for Windows' folder is labeled winword. These folders will probably be either at the C:\ root level or inside the Windows folder. If you see a folder you don't understand, leave it where it is for now. Later, as you use your PC more, you may discover that the folder contains a program that belongs in the Apps folder.

> IMPORTANT: Before you proceed to the next step, be aware of an important warning. If these programs have already been installed under Windows (and icons for these programs exist in the Program Manager), the Program Manager icons will lose track of the program files when you move the folders around—which the next step does. We'll take care of this problem in the next Encounter. If you must use the computer or programs between now and the completion of the next Encounter, stop here. You need to perform the rest of this Encounter and the next Encounter at one sitting.

3. Drag these folders into the Apps folder.

4. Resize the File Manager's panes approximately as shown in figure 8.17.

Figure 8.17
*Typical File
Manager window
for the new
organization.*

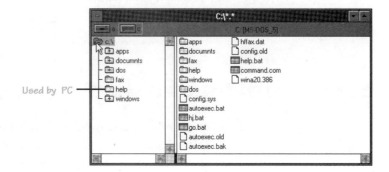

5. Double-click the control menu box in the File Manager window to exit the File Manager.

Summary

In this encounter, you've learned how to manipulate folders and files to create an effective organization method for the documents we'll be creating.

Exorcises

1. The File Manager lets us organize files into iconic folders, each of which is called a(n) _____.

2. The left pane of the File Manager displays the _____.

3. What can you determine about the contents of the letters folder in figure 8.18?

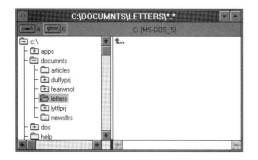

Figure 8.18
What's in the Letters folder?

4. How do you drag a file to a folder you cannot see in the directory tree diagram?

5. In figure 8.19, the intention is to move the selected file to the Documnts folder. According to the indications in the illustration, what will happen if the user releases the mouse button right now? What should the user have done instead?

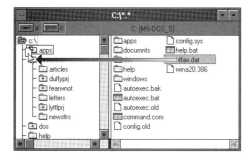

Figure 8.19
What happens at the mouse button release now?

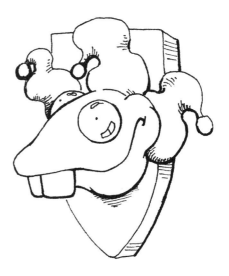

9th Encounter

Getting Organized— Programs

Goal

To set up a practical Program Manager window layout (and fix anything we may have broken in the last Encounter) so that we can get to programs quickly.

What You Will Need

PC turned on with Windows running.

Terms of Enfearment

properties	working directory
command line	tiled windows
Browse button	cascading windows

Briefing

A Fine Mess

Before we start playing around with the Program Manager again, it's important to know how to clear up any problems that may have grown out of our File Manager organization in the previous Encounter. At the core of our problem are the program item icons, which won't be able to find the programs that we moved into the Apps folder. This problem is relevant only to application programs we've moved to the Apps folder, not to things like Windows accessories or other items that come with Windows (most of the stuff in the Main group).

A program item icon in the Program Manager has a series of *properties*, another way of saying that each one has a set of characteristics that helps define what that icon does for us. To view a program item's properties, select the item and choose Properties from the File menu (see fig. 9.1). Because you may be doing a lot of this property stuff now, you can use the speedcut of holding down the Alt key and double-clicking the item icon.

Figure 9.1

Select an icon and open its properties.

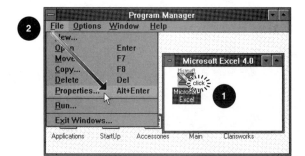

Hot Properties

In the resulting dialog box are several fields that define important elements about that icon (see fig. 9.2). First is the description—the label assigned to the icon. Because we're not naming a DOS file—but simply a representation of a file—we're not limited to the DOS file-naming structure. Go nuts: you've got 40 characters to describe the item in language that helps you identify the item on sight.

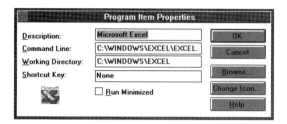

Figure 9.2
The Properties dialog box for a selected program item.

In the next field is the *command line.* This is another case of DOS-in-your-face. A command line is the text command we would have to type from the DOS C:\> prompt to start the program (the program item icon essentially does this for us when we double-click it). Because we've moved the program to another directory, the original path for the program is no longer valid. Before going on, however, it's a good idea to jot down the name of the file at the end of the line, because we must find it on the hard disk in the next step (see fig. 9.3).

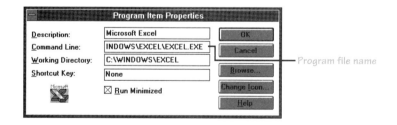

Figure 9.3
The last item in the line is the program file name.

Just Browsing, Thanks

Fortunately, we don't have to type a thing into this field. The *Browse button* in this dialog lets us use another dialog box to locate the program in a File Manager-like view (see fig. 9.4). We'll sort through the details of this dialog box in a later Encounter, but for now, we just need to know how to get to our applications. Double-clicking on the c:\ folder gets our view to the root level, from where we can open the Apps folder and then whatever program folder we're looking for. The dialog box is filtering the view of files (on the left) so that we see only programs or files that can start programs. Locate the file that has the name you jotted down, click on that file name, and click the OK button. The full path is now in the field.

Figure 9.4
Using the Browse dialog to locate a program for the Properties dialog.

The next field in the Properties dialog, *working directory*, also consists of a pathname. A working directory is the folder that appears as the first place to store documents we create with the program. If the property is from the program's original installation on your PC, the working directory is the same as the program's original folder. This won't help organize your documents. We've set up a Documnts folder for that.

Unfortunately, we have to type this pathname into the working directory field. The good news is that it isn't very long: *c:\documnts*. This pathname belongs in every program's working directory property.

Our Computer Dashboard

Although the File Manager shows us in painstaking detail everything about our hard disk's contents, the Program Manager lets us see and organize only those items we need everyday. Therefore, even if a program we use has a dozen component files in its real folder on the hard disk, we can reduce this all to a single pretty icon in the Program Manager. It's much like an automobile dashboard, which lets us work with only the items everyone needs day-to-day (lights, wipers, fuel level, and so on), but under the hood, a knowledgeable person can get down to the nitty gritty (spark plug gaps, carburetor adjustment, transmission fluid level, and so on).

Refresher

We saw earlier that the Program Manager display consists only of *group icons*. Each one of these icons expands to a window, which may contain any number of *program item icons* that represent programs or document files.

Program item icons may not be dragged to the white space of the Program Manager window. The inconvenience of this limitation is that if we follow standard procedure, we would be opening and closing group windows all day long to get to our programs.

A Windows program you install typically places its own group icon in the Program Manager window as part of its automatic installation process (see fig. 9.5). This might lead you to think that a group icon for each program is the prescribed way to use the Program Manager. Wrong!

Figure 9.5

Programs typically install their own group icons in the Program Manager.

What's the Right Way?

There is no right or wrong way to set up the Program Manager, but some ways are more efficient than others. The goal for any scheme should be to provide you with the quickest access to stuff you use every day.

I advocate reducing the number of group icons to a minimum: Applications and Startup. The quickest way to accomplish this is to place all applications (Windows and DOS programs, accessories, and Windows utilities) into a single group and to leave that group open at all times. You can use the

Applications group shown in figure 9.6 that Windows automatically created upon installation or rename it as you like. The programs that Windows automatically installs there(QBasic, Now, MS-DOS Editor) are for wire-heads, so feel free to select each one and to choose Delete from the File menu. If someone needs those programs, they're still on the hard disk and can be activated or even re-installed into the Program Manager later. We'll get into the Startup group in a later Encounter.

Figure 9.6

My favorite method gives me ready access to all programs.

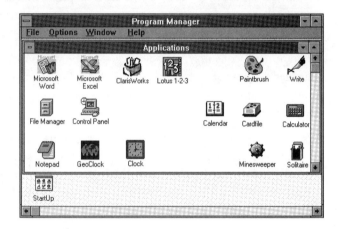

Moving Items

Just like moving stuff around the File Manager, we drag icons from group to group in the Program Manager (see fig. 9.7). For example, to move the items from the Accessories group to the Applications group, do the following:

1. Open the Accessories window.

2. Make sure that the Applications group icon is visible.

3. Drag each item you want from the Accessories window to the Applications group icon.

When all items are out of the Accessories window, close the window, select the Accessories group icon, and choose Delete from the File menu.

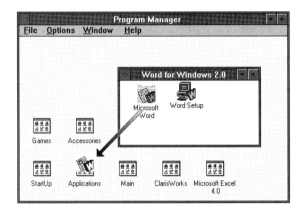

Figure 9.7

Dragging a program item from one open group to another group's icon.

To the Max

Because we now have essentially one window, we can maximize it to take over the entire Program Manager window (we'll rarely need access to the Startup group). Leave this group open at all times. Another helpful hint is to manually organize the items in this window to help you find them (see fig. 9.8). As an example, you can place all frequently used programs in the top or bottom row of icons. Visual grouping of related items is a valuable organizational tool.

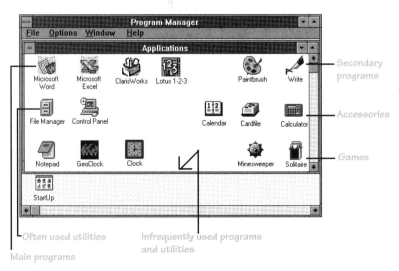

Figure 9.8

Organizing icons within the group window helps you find items more quickly.

Other Ideas

Of course, no one is insisting you use this Program Manager method.

One alternative is to create two applications groups—one each for primary (day-to-day) applications and those you don't use very often. You then may want to arrange the windows with the help of the Tile and Cascade commands in the Window menu. With both windows open, choose either command. *Tiled windows* are sized to allow you to see equal amounts of each window without any overlapping (see fig. 9.9); *cascading windows* overlap in an orderly fashion, making it relatively easy to click a specific window to bring it to the front (see fig. 9.10).

Figure 9.9
Tiled windows.

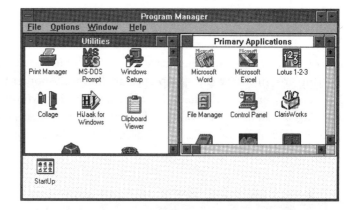

Figure 9.10
Cascading windows.

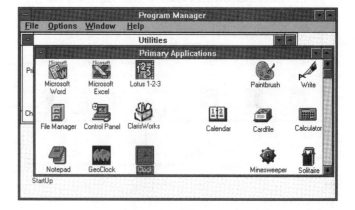

New Items

Because any file can become a program item, we can set up documents inside groups as well. While in the Program Manager, choose New from the File menu. In the New Program Object dialog box, click the Program Item button and OK. The Program Item Properties dialog box appears (see fig. 9.11). Use the Browse button to locate the file you would like represented in the group (change file types to "All Files" to see documents). Be sure to give the item a descriptive name. As long as the document's path is in the command line, Windows takes care of the Working Directory information.

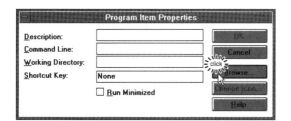

Figure 9.11

Using the Browse button to locate a file when creating a program item icon for a document.

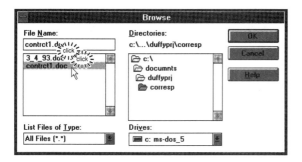

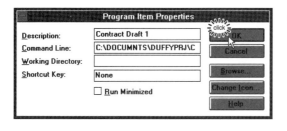

Document Groups

Because we can also bring document icons into the Program Manager, it may be convenient to have items representing templates or forms you use all the time. You also may want to create a temporary group containing a number of documents (created with different applications) pertaining to an active project on which you're working (see fig. 9.12). Again, you can elect to tile or cascade the windows.

Figure 9.12
A project-oriented group window.

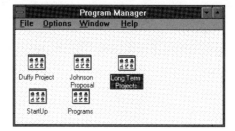

Whatever scheme you use (and don't be afraid to change schemes as the need arises), try to keep the number of groups to a minimum and then leave those windows open. The more you have to double-click group icons to open windows before gaining access to an item, the more that Windows gets in your productive way.

They're Out To Get Us

The error messages Windows provides when the Command line or Working Directory properties aren't valid (i.e., after you move stuff around) can cause your heart to skip a beat (see fig. 9.13). In reality, the messages are merely advising of invalid paths. Nothing terrible is about to happen, except that the icon may not be able to open the program if the path is wrong. When either of these messages appears, head straight to the Properties dialog box for the program item and fix the paths.

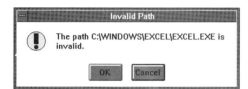

Figure 9.13
*Alerts that tell us
about invalid paths.*

If you've carefully arranged the icons in a group window, *do not* choose Arrange Icons from the Window menu; nor should you turn on Auto Arrange in the Options menu. These commands try to fit icons in as few rows as possible, within the size of your window. Your careful visual organizing will be wiped out—and there's no undo.

One problem with placing document icons in the Program Manager is that double-clicking a document usually starts a second copy of the program running—eating up valuable memory and other system resources.

Practice

Viewing Properties

1. Double-click the Accessories group icon.

2. Click the Write program item icon.

3. Choose Properties from the File menu (see fig. 9.14). Items that are created when Windows installs itself do not have any Working Directory information filled in, in which case Windows uses its own folder as the working directory.

Figure 9.14

Write's Properties dialog box.

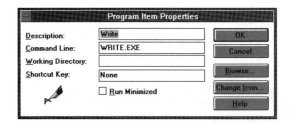

4. Click the Cancel button to close the window without making any changes.

Setting Working Directories

Perform the following steps only if you have set up a Documnts folder as detailed in the previous Encounter.

1. Open the Properties dialog for Write again.

2. Press the Tab key twice so that the flashing cursor appears in the Working Directory field. (If there is information in this field from a previous user, the text highlights—which is also fine for our purposes.)

3. Type *c:\documnts* into the field as shown in figure 9.15 (note the backslash and the fact that the eight-character folder name makes us spell documents without the "e").

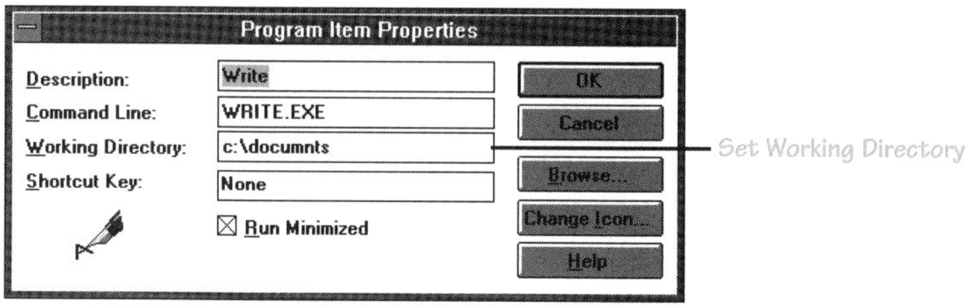

Figure 9.15

Write's Properties dialog modified to show the documnts folder as the default location for storing document files.

4. Click the OK button or press the Enter key. If you made a typing error, a message will tell you that the Working Directory is not valid. Click the Cancel button and check your typing.

Setting Command Lines

Perform these steps only if you moved applications programs into the Apps folder, as detailed in the previous Encounter. Repeat these steps for each application program for which you have icons in the Program Manager.

1. Open the Properties dialog box for an application program icon.

2. Click the Browse button.

3. Double-click the c:\ folder in the right pane to view all folders at the root level.

4. Double-click the Apps folder to view all folders of applications you've moved to that folder.

5. Double-click the folder for the application whose icon you're adjusting.

6. Double-click the name of the program file (it usually has an extension of "exe"). The complete path for that file goes into the Command Line field.

7. Click the OK button or press the Enter key to record the change.

Deleting Program Items

1. Open the Applications group window.

2. Unless you know you need the QBasic, Now, and MS-DOS Editor, select one of them.

3. Choose Delete from the File menu. In response to the warning dialog box, click the OK button.

4. Repeat steps 2 and 3 for all other items in the Applications window that you don't need.

5. Close the Applications window by double-clicking the control menu button.

Moving Program Items

1. Open the Accessories group window and resize it so that you can also see the Applications group icon.

2. Drag and drop each accessory icon to the Applications group icon.

3. When the Accessories window is empty, close it.

4. Repeat steps 1 through 3 for items in the Main group and any application-specific group (e.g., Word for Windows).

5. Open the Applications window to see the results of the drags.

Deleting Group Icons

1. Select a group icon for any group you emptied in the preceding steps.

2. Choose Delete from the File menu. In response to the warning, click the OK button.

3. Repeat steps 1 and 2 for all empty groups until you have only the Applications and Startup group icons left.

Summary

You now have a practical arrangement of your Program Manager, which acts like a dashboard to your programs.

Exorcises

1. The Program Manager displays two kinds of icons. One, called a _____, represents a minimized window of one or more icons. The other, called a _____, represents programs and documents we choose to have handy on the desktop.

2. A program item's icon lets us view its attributes by choosing _____ from the File menu.

3. Explain the differences between the Working Directory and Command Line fields of a Properties dialog box.

Staying Organized

Goal

Learn skills important to maintaining an organized
hard disk and Windows environment, including
ways of finding deeply nested files and of clearing
away unneeded files.

What You Will Need

PC turned on with Windows running.

Terms of Enfearment

search	copying files
wildcards	deleting files

Briefing

"Where's That #&%* File?"

When a hard disk gets lots of files and folders stored on it, we can use the File Manager to help us locate a particular file. We must know at least part of the file's name before we can send the File Manager on its safari.

In the File menu is a *Search* command, which leads to the Search dialog box. In the first field is a strange construction: *.* (see fig. 10.1). This brings us to another DOS-related discussion about wildcards.

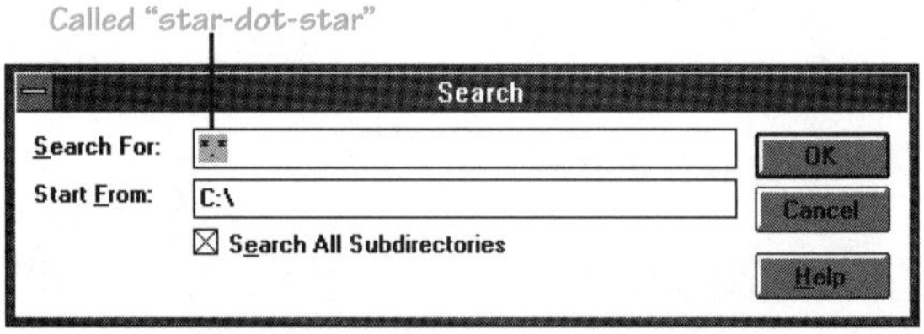

Figure 10.1

The Search dialog and the weird ".*" symbol.*

Called "star-dot-star"

Asterisks Are Wild

Sometimes, you don't remember exactly how you named a file, but you may remember how many characters it has. When you're not sure of a character, DOS lets you substitute a question mark for it. DOS considers a question mark to be any character—like a *wildcard* in poker. Therefore, the search for a file name of *bla?e* would find files named *blade*, *blake*, and *blase* if they existed. A question mark stands in for just one character. If you don't know two characters, place a question mark in each location. A search for *bla??* would locate the three found before, plus *black* and *bland*.

When you don't know the number of characters or any part of the file name or extension, you can use one asterisk symbol to take up the slack. For example, **.exe* means all files that have an exe extension; *budget.** means all files named *budget* regardless of extension. See Table 10.1 for examples of searching with the asterisk wildcard.

Table 10.1. Searching with Wildcards

Search for	Finds	But not
*.doc	memo.doc letter12.doc	memo.wrt, doc.xls
memo.*	memo.doc, memo.pif	memo9.doc
me*.doc	me.doc, memo.doc, memo12.doc	me.bat, memo.lgo, memo12.wri
.	all files	—

Time To Type

The File Manager is kind of particular about what we type in the Search dialog. For example, if the file we're looking for is named memo.doc, we can't just type *me* and expect the File Manager to locate the file, even though the file starts with those characters. We would have to at least type the full word "memo." If we type one word like that, the File Manager considers the word to be the total file name (with a wildcard extension understood).

Start Searching Where?

The second field in the Search dialog displays a path that indicates the starting point of the search. Although we can type a path if we like, we can also help this field along *before* choosing Search from the File menu; select the directory in the File Manager tree diagram first (see fig. 10.2). The more we can narrow the scope of the search—by starting from a nested folder and entering as much of the file name as we can remember, the faster the search will be.

Figure 10.2

Click a starting directory before choosing Search.

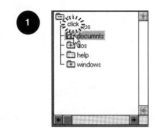

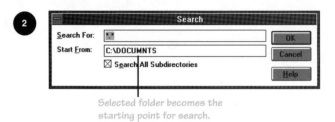

Selected folder becomes the
starting point for search.

Eureka!

When the File Manager locates one or more matches for your search criteria,
it presents a Search Results window (see fig. 10.3). Parts of the View menu
remain active for a Search Results window so that we can see the list of files,
their sizes, dates, and so on.

Figure 10.3

The Search Results window.

Two matches found —

Search for files with xls extension
starting from C:\DOCUMNTS

Interestingly, the Results window also includes a minimize button. Clicking
it causes an icon representing that window to appear at the bottom of the
File Manager window (see fig. 10.4). Therefore, we can keep a view of
selected files handy if we need to refer to it frequently (although the search
won't be updated automatically to reflect additions to our hard disk).

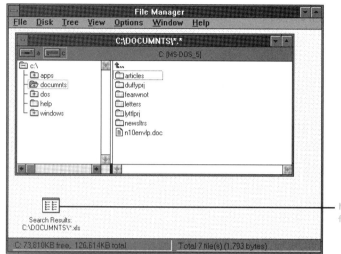

Figure 10.4
*Minimize the Search
Results window for a
handy reference.*

Minimized results window
from figure 10.3

Copying Files

In all the dragging of files and folders up to now, all we were doing was
moving items around. When we're all done, there is still a single copy of
each file on the disk. We can, however, make a copy of a file on the hard
disk—in two ways.

The inefficient method is one you don't have to remember, because the
menus help you out. Select a file and choose Copy from the File menu. A
dialog comes up asking you to type a pathname for the copy of the file (see
fig. 10.5). This is a lot of typing, so it will be worth it to remember the
following magic sequence.

Figure 10.5

The easy-to-find, but slow, way to copy a file.

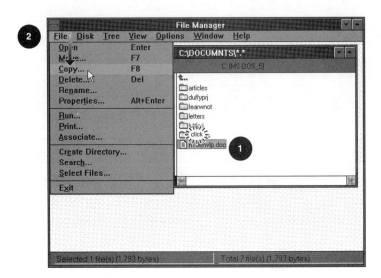

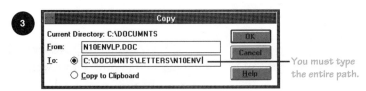

You must type the entire path.

Copying Like Magic

When the copy of a file we're making is supposed to go into another folder on the same hard disk, there's a speedcut. Hold down the Control key while dragging an item from one folder to another (see fig. 10.6). As we drag the icon to another folder, its little document icon shows a plus symbol, meaning that the file will be copied (not moved) to that other folder. Release the mouse button, and the File Manager duplicates the selected file and puts the copy—with the exact name as the original in the destination.

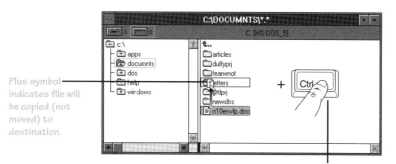

Figure 10.6
Control-dragging is the convenient, speedy way to copy a file to another folder or drive.

Plus symbol indicates file will be copied (not moved) to destination.

Hold down Ctrl key while dragging.

It is possible to move and copy more than one file at a time, but all the source files must be in the same folder. With that source folder selected in the tree diagram, Control-click on each file in the right pane to be copied. Then Control-drag any one of the files as shown in figure 10.7—they all go as a group (and the icon we drag turns into a multiple-page document icon).

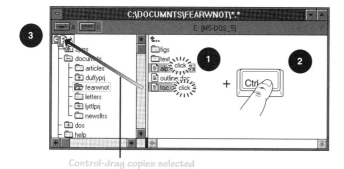

Figure 10.7
Control-click on multiple files and then Control-drag the items to another folder.

Control-drag copies selected files to destination.

We're more likely to want to make a copy of a file or folder for storage on another hard disk, file server, or even a floppy disk volume.

Deleting Files

The hard disk is not a bottomless pit into which we can throw thousands of files. Eventually, it becomes necessary to remove some files. When we no longer need a file, we select it (or Control-select any number of files in a folder) and choose Delete from the File menu. Two alert messages ask us to confirm the deletion.

In the second alert is an extra button, labeled `Yes to All` (see fig. 10.8). This button is active if we've selected multiple files for deletion. Clicking this button confirms that we want to delete everything we've selected and that we don't want to be bothered with an extra alert message for each file.

Figure 10.8

The `Yes to All`
*button activates if
you've selected
multiple files for
deletion.*

They're Out To Get Us

Before clicking the OK and Yes buttons in the file deletion alert messages in Windows, always read the message carefully. Double-check that the file you've selected is in the desired folder—the File Manager can't read your mind. The phrase, "I didn't mean that one, too!" falls on deaf chips.

After you've deleted a file, nothing that comes with Windows will dig a file out of the dumpster. DOS 5 and later comes with a rudimentary file recovery utility, but its operation may be complex unless you're very conversant with DOS. Some commercial software programs, however, can make file recovery a bit easier. (The file isn't erased; only its entry in the hard disk's internal table of contents is erased.) Popular utilities include Norton Utilities (Symantec Corp.) and PC Tools (Central Point Software).

Practice

Unsuccessful Search

1. Choose Search from the File menu.

2. Enter ABC123 on the Search For line in the dialog box and press Enter (the same as clicking the highlighted Find button in the dialog). An alert box tells of an unsuccessful search (see fig. 10.9). Click OK.

Figure 10.9
Searching for ABC123.

A Successful Search

1. Click the c:\ folder in the directory tree diagram.

2. Choose Search from the File menu.

3. Enter *win.com* and press Enter. The File Manager lists the win.com file from the Windows folder (see fig. 10.10).

Figure 10.10

A successful search found one file to match.

Found file

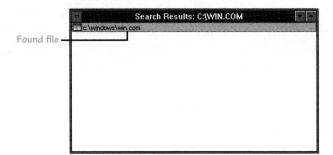

4. Close the Search Results window.

Wildcard Searching

1. Search for the exe extension by using "*.exe" to locate all programs on your hard disk (including utility and accessory programs).

2. Minimize the Search Results window.

3. Double-click the minimized window to restore it.

4. Search for "win*.*" to locate all files that start with the characters "win" and that have any kind of extension.

5. Close the Search Results window after you've studied the list of items that the File Manager found.

Duplicating an Item

1. Create a folder at the root level and name it *Encntr10*.

2. While holding down the Control key, drag the *Encntr10* folder onto the Apps folder. This action duplicates the folder and places the copy into the Apps folder.

3. Open the Apps folder to see the results of the option-drag.

4. Close the Apps folder.

More Searching

1. Click the C:\ directory in the tree.

2. Choose Search from the File menu, enter *Encntr10*, and press Enter.

3. In figure 10.11, notice the two different paths to the Encntr10 folders that Windows found.

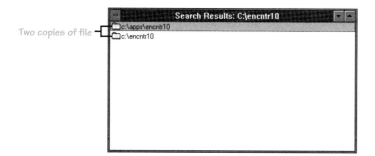

Figure 10.11

The search found items in two directories.

Deleting Folders (Works for Files, Too)

1. Control-click the two folders in the Search Results window to select both folders.

2. Choose Delete from the File menu.

3. In response to the confirmation dialogs, click the Yes to All button.

4. A dialog reminds you that the hard disk's contents have changed and that the results of the search may be affected (see fig. 10.12). Click the Yes button.

Figure 10.12

The deletion may affect the contents of the Search Results window.

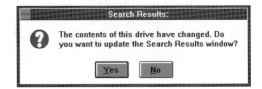

5. Notice that the Search Results window empties, because no other file or folder meets the search criteria for this window.

Summary

The File Manager contains facilities that let us search our hard disk(s) for files or folders whose exact locations we don't remember. We saw the difference between moving files around a volume and making copies of them on the same volume, including the Control-drag-and-drop shortcut for placing a copy of a file into another folder. Files and folders may be removed from the hard disk by first selecting their icons in the File Manager and then choosing Delete from the File menu. Deletions can also be performed from a Search Results window.

Exorcises

1. Describe the fastest way to place a copy of a file into another folder.

2. Your hard disk is getting full, and you want to open up some space. Detail the steps you would go through to accomplish this.

3. You want to archive all the work you have done today by copying those files to another drive (whose icon appears in the File Manager window). What would be the most expedient way to accomplish this?

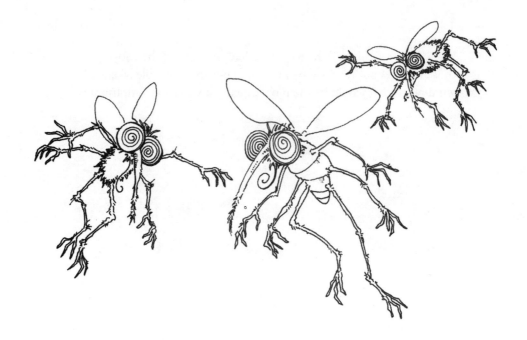

Starting a Program

Goal

Become acquainted with ways to start a program, learn how to switch between multiple programs for maximum efficiency, and recognize which program is running at any moment.

What You Will Need

PC turned on with Windows running. A program called Write installed on your hard disk (the Windows installation process does this for you).

Terms of Enfearment

program	launch
application	application window
utility	document window
applet	palette
boot (again)	toolbar
load	Task List

Briefing

Programs and Us

Everything we've learned so far is vital to using Windows, but little of it has anything to do with the work we do. What turns the PC into a practical tool for our daily labors is a *program*. Each program transforms the collection of computer parts into a special purpose tool for writing, massaging budgets, organizing information, drawing—virtually everything that involves knowledge, facts, or ideas.

The terms *program* and *application* are often used interchangeably, the latter sounding less computer-like. Sometimes, the terms are used together, as in *application program*, to distinguish an application from other kinds of programs (for example, a *utility program* that backs up a hard disk). Gurus usually shorten the word *application* to just plain *app*.

Two Program Types (Sort Of)

Some Windows experts classify Windows "accessories" as a category distinct from full-fledged applications programs. Some even refer to these programs as *applets*—if Windows were a modern kiddy cartoon series, they would be called Application Babies. But, we've lumped these accessories and applications into one category of programs.

Full-fledged applications are the ones that we use for our real work. They're the word processors, spreadsheets, databases, communications, and graphics programs that help us cope with all kinds of information.

Commercial programs arrive on floppy disks. To use a program, you usually copy it to the hard disk, often by way of an automatic installer (installation instructions vary from program to program). When installed on your hard disk, the program consists of one or more files, one of which is the one you start from the File Manager or Program Manager.

Starting an Application

Although starting an application is easy, remembering all the terms for it may not be. You'll hear phrases like *booting* or *loading* the program and *launching* the app (or any combination). They all mean the same thing: starting the application.

Starting an application is as easy as double-clicking on the program's icon in the Program Manager or File Manager. This action is the same as selecting the icon and choosing Open from the File menu (see fig. 11.1). (Here's another way to describe the action: *opening* an application.)

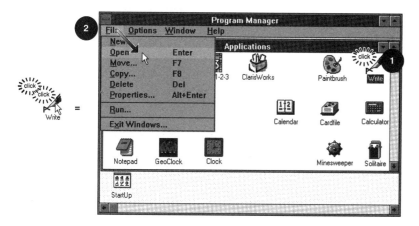

Figure 11.1

Opening an application by double-clicking its icon or selecting the icon and using the File menu.

A program occupies its own window, called, aptly enough, the *application window*. That window has a menu bar specific to that program. Inside that program window space (which, like all windows, is resizable), the program may allow one or more *document windows*, where we do most of the work (see fig. 11.2).

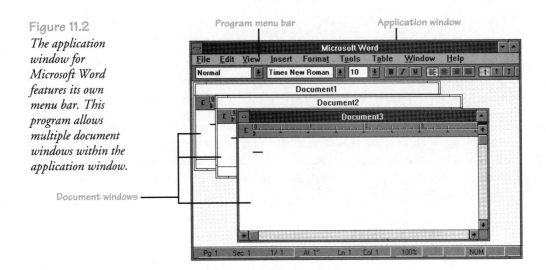

Figure 11.2

The application window for Microsoft Word features its own menu bar. This program allows multiple document windows within the application window.

Program Behavior

When a program starts up, it generally produces one blank (untitled) window inside its own window. Some programs also display one or more additional smaller windows, called *palettes* (see fig. 11.3). Found more in graphics-oriented programs, palettes contain tools that let us switch between types of operations, such as typing text, drawing circles, or dragging chunks of our work around the window. The precise functions of palettes vary from program to program, and the palette window style may also vary, but you can drag them around by their title bars and close them by clicking their close boxes, just like windows we've seen earlier.

An increasingly popular feature appearing in program screens is the *toolbar*. It usually extends across the window just below the menu bar (see fig. 11.4). Toolbars display icons that represent frequently used pull-down menu commands. We can click them as a speedcut to dragging through a menu.

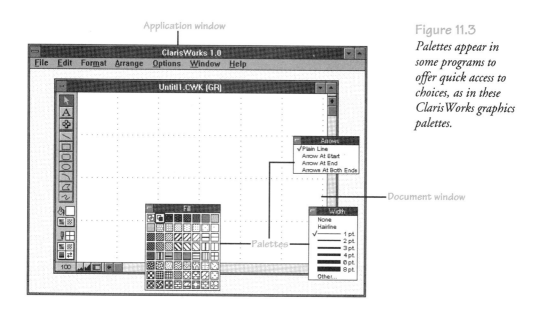

Figure 11.3
Palettes appear in some programs to offer quick access to choices, as in these ClarisWorks graphics palettes.

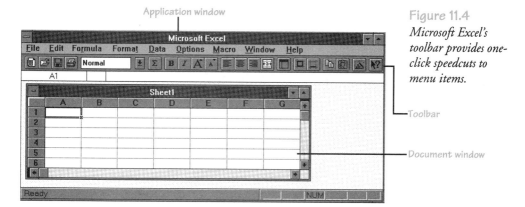

Figure 11.4
Microsoft Excel's toolbar provides one-click speedcuts to menu items.

Using Multiple Programs

Windows accommodates as many programs as the machine has available RAM space (including virtual memory, as discussed in the 7th Encounter). Each program takes up a different amount of RAM, depending on capabilities of the program and the skills of the program's designers.

Even though more than one program can be open, only one can be the active program—the one whose window is the active window. Other programs may actually be performing some action in the background (such as sending a file to another computer over the telephone), but only one application can be on top of the pile visually.

If the screen is cluttered with windows, and you're not sure which programs are currently running, you can see a list of all open programs. The list comes in a window called the *Task List*. The quickest way to bring up the Task List window is to double-click anywhere on the background desktop, if it's visible (see fig. 11.5). Otherwise, the keyboard sequence Control-Escape brings up the window.

Figure 11.5
Double-click the desktop background to display the Task List window.

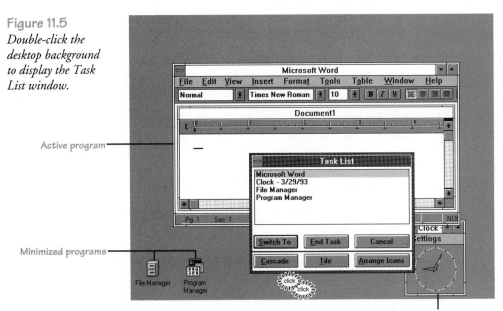

This window serves multiple duties, as well. The highlighted item in the list is the active application at that moment. Double-clicking another item switches to that program. We can also use the other buttons there to arrange the windows of all open programs in either cascading or tiled arrangement.

Quick Switching

We can bypass the Task List with another magical keyboard sequence that is worth remembering: holding down the Alt key and repeatedly pressing the Tab key. Each press of the Tab key displays in a special dialog box the next open program in sequence (see fig. 11.6). When the desired program name is displayed in the box, release the Alt key, and Windows switches to that application. Switching between applications doesn't affect the contents of any work going on in that application, but it's a good idea to save the current state of the document before switching (more about this in the 13th Encounter).

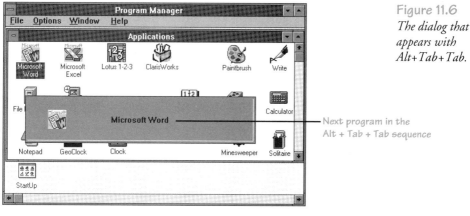

Next program in the
Alt + Tab + Tab sequence

Figure 11.6
The dialog that appears with Alt+Tab+Tab.

They're Out To Get Us

Although I said earlier that you can click on an inactive program's window to activate that program, it is possible that one program's window will become totally hidden by another application's window. That's not really a problem, because you can use the Task List—or better yet, the Alt+Tab sequence—to make that otherwise hidden window come to the top of the pile.

A Clean Screen

If things get too confusing on the screen with all kinds of applications showing, click the minimize button in the program's window. This doesn't quit the program—it just temporarily shrinks it to an icon on the desktop. Double-click the icon to zoom a minimized program up to regular size in a flash.

Starting DOS Applications— Big Deal!

The Windows manual (and other Windows books) spill a lot of ink about running DOS (non-Windows) programs from Windows. Technically, this is an amazing feat, but we should consider it no more than running another program with some slightly different behavior.

DOS programs typically don't install themselves into the Program Manager when they're set up. But it's easy enough to do. After the program has been installed to the hard disk (following the program's installation instructions), open the Program Manager group window where you want this program's icon to be. Then choose New from the File menu and select the program item choice.

Next, use the Browse button to locate the program file. Program files usually have the extension exe and sometimes com. More recent DOS programs, however, include a file with the pif extension—a *program information file* that Windows uses to great advantage. Included in that pif file is a specially designed pretty icon for the Program Manager. If you see a pif file in the program's folder, this is the file to open via the Browse dialog (see fig. 11.7); otherwise, choose the exe or com file.

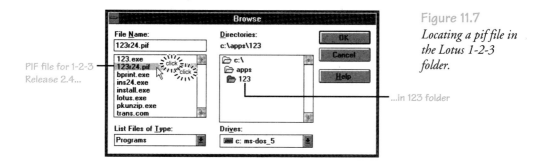

PIF file for 1-2-3
Release 2.4...

...in 123 folder

Figure 11.7
Locating a pif file in the Lotus 1-2-3 folder.

After a DOS program has an icon in the Program Manager, we start it like any Windows program—by double-clicking the icon. But here's where things may get tricky.

Running DOS Programs

Most DOS programs open up to occupy the entire video screen, completely obscuring anything vaguely resembling the Windows environment. If we quit the DOS program, we're brought back into Windows where we left off. But, we can also switch between Windows and DOS programs just like we switched between multiple Windows programs: by pressing Alt+Tab+Tab.

Holding down the Alt key and pressing Tab a few times cycles through the open applications appearing in a narrow banner across the top of the screen. This banner behaves just like the Alt+Tab+Tab window that appears in the Windows environment. Release the Alt key when the desired program's name appears in the banner.

Back in Windows, the DOS program minimizes itself to an icon on the Desktop.

Practice

Starting an Application

1. Locate the Write icon in your Program Manager's Applications window (if you've set up the Program Manager as detailed in the 9th Encounter).

2. Double-click the Write icon. The program's window appears and becomes the active program.

Switching among Programs

1. Minimize the Write program.

2. Open the Calculator program.

3. Hold down the Alt key and press the Tab key slowly a few times. Notice how the open programs (including the Program Manager and, if open, the File Manager) appear in the dialog box in a predictable rotation—Calculator, File Manager, Write (see fig. 11.8).

Figure 11.8

Open programs appear in rotation with each Alt+Tab.

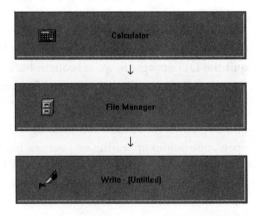

4. With Write showing in the dialog, release the Alt key. The Write program window zooms back to its previous size.

5. Switch among the various open programs in this manner several times.

Switching with the Task List

1. Double-click anywhere on the desktop space. The Task List window appears, with the active program highlighted (see fig. 11.9).

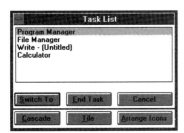

Figure 11.9
The Task List window.

2. Double-click one of the other programs to make it the active program. The Task List window goes away after you make a selection.

Installing a DOS Program

1. Open the Program Manager and the Applications group.

2. Choose New from the File menu and click the program item button before clicking OK.

3. In the Program Item Properties dialog, click the Browse button.

4. Locate and select the edit.pif file in the Windows folder. Figure 11.10 shows the pif file for the MS-DOS Editor (which you may have deleted from the Program Manager in the 10th Encounter).

5. Click OK in the Program Item Properties dialog. For major DOS programs, the pif file includes a pretty icon and description, which are automatically applied to the program item.

Figure 11.10
*MS-DOS Editor
doesn't have its own
icon, so Windows
installs a generic
DOS icon.*

MS-DOS
Editor

Running a DOS Program

1. Double-click the MS-DOS Editor program icon. The program occupies the entire screen, hiding everything in Windows.

2. Hold down the Alt key and press the Tab key until the Program Manager shows in the banner atop the screen. Then release the Alt key. Notice that MS-DOS Editor is now a minimized icon on the Windows desktop.

3. Press Alt+Tab again until the MS-DOS Editor shows in the dialog and release the Alt key.

4. Press the Escape key to clear the program's welcome screen.

5. Type the following keyboard sequence to quit the program: Alt, F, X.

Summary

You can open as many programs as your Windows environment has available RAM and then freely switch between programs as you need them. Most DOS programs run comfortably inside Windows, and you can install DOS programs into the Program Manager for easy access.

Exorcises

1. How do you start an application from the Program Manager?

2. How many programs can you open in a PC equipped with 4 MB of RAM?

3. What is the most efficient way to switch from one open program to another?

4. Describe two ways to determine which among four open applications is the active program.

5. You want to install a program icon for Lotus 1-2-3 for DOS into your Program Manager. Given the contents of the 123 folder shown in figure 11.11, what steps would you follow to complete the installation?

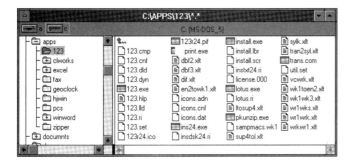

Figure 11.11
How would you complete installation of Lotus 1-2-3 into your Program Manager?

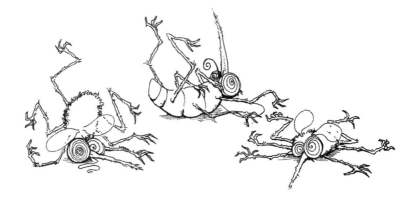

12th Encounter

Where the Action Is: The Document Window

Goal

Examine where we do the real work with the computer—the document window.

What You Will Need

Where we left the 11th Encounter, with the PC turned on and with Write open.

Terms of Enfearment

document   graphics program
document window   database
spreadsheet

Briefing

Document Terminology

Unless you dwell in the Realm of Pure Thought, your work produces something tangible. Perhaps it's on paper, from a tiny doodle to a multi-volume encyclopedia; perhaps the work ultimately becomes a color slide for a presentation; it may even be an audio or video tape of material you or others recorded. To Windows, each chunk of work, stored on the hard disk as a separate file, is called a *document.*

The less a program replicates printed documents from the real world, the more likely it will have its own terminology for a document. For example, a document that contains a video sequence may be called a *movie* or a *clip* in a video-editing program. Such naming helps users experienced with those terms make the connection between the real world and what's taking place on the PC. To Windows, however, a document is a document, regardless of its content.

The Document Workplace

All work on a document takes place in a *document window.* The precise look of a document window varies widely with the application. It may be a completely blank canvas for drawing, a grid of rectangles for entering numbers in a ledger-like sheet, or a well-defined form that needs to be filled out blank-by-blank. In designing Windows document windows, a program's creator usually tries to replicate in electronic form something familiar from the real world.

A New Document

When most programs start, they present either a new, untitled document window or an empty workspace. This is the equivalent of the dreaded blank sheet of paper lying before you on the desk. Despite powerful tools available in the program, it is up to us to do the next step: put something into the document.

Text Entry

Any document that expects lots of text (e.g., word processing) awaits typing from the keyboard. A flashing text insertion pointer tells us that the next characters we type on the keyboard will go where the pointer is flashing (see fig. 12.1). Setting margins, line spacing, and other attributes of the document are left to menu commands or toolbar clicks.

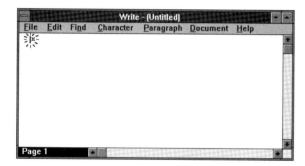

Figure 12.1

In this word processing window, the text insertion pointer flashes where the next character we type will appear (MS-Word for Windows).

Numbers, Numbers, Numbers

Spreadsheet programs are popular because they present a structured way of organizing figures, as if on accounting paper. Each rectangle is called a cell, which can contain a raw number or a calculation formula to be performed on raw numbers of other cells (e.g., the total for a column of figures). In place of the text insertion pointer is a cell selection rectangle, which highlights the cell whose contents are to be changed. Spreadsheet data entry is stranger than most, because you type into a text entry area near the top of the window (see fig. 12.2). Only when you press the Tab or Enter key does what you type officially get entered into the selected cell.

Figure 12.2

*Entry of information
into spreadsheet cells
is usually by way of a
data-entry field
(MS-Excel).*

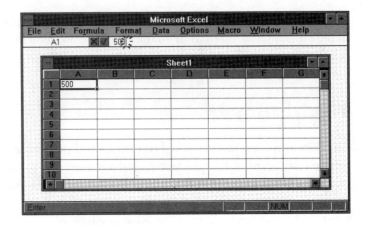

A Thousand Words

The specifics about working with *graphics programs* vary widely from program to program. But one basic methodology holds for nearly all of them:
you choose a tool from a palette; the pointer becomes that tool; and you
then start drawing in the document window with that tool. One tool might
draw straight lines, and another draws ovals filled with color patterns (see fig.
12.3). There is no insertion pointer or selected cell—we control every aspect
of a shape's location with the mouse-controlled pointer.

Figure 12.3

*In this Paintbrush
document, we choose
a tool (round
rectangle) and then
drag the shape with
the mouse.*

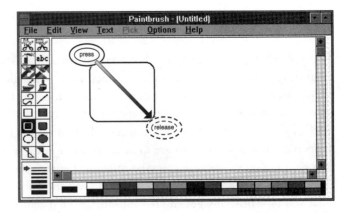

A Base of Data

At many times in our lives, we've kept lists of information. The data may have been so voluminous as to require a shoe box full of index cards or short enough to be written on a small note paper in our wallets. The larger a collection of data becomes, the more helpful a computer is for it, because the computer is quick at sorting and finding what we want. There are two parts to a *database* program: designing the database and entering and working with information in the database. The former is the more difficult of the tasks but is required before any information may be entered (see fig. 12.4). After the database is set up, however, it is a piece of cake to enter additional information into the database's on-screen forms (see fig. 12.5) and to extract information based on selection criteria (e.g., all sales prospects whose telephone numbers contain the 212 area code).

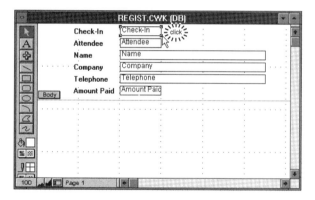

Figure 12.4
Before we enter info into a database, we must design a form layout, with each field's name, location, and size (ClarisWorks).

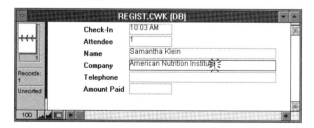

Figure 12.5
After the layout is set, we can begin filling in data.

If You Don't Know How To Start

If you come to a program and you're at a loss about what to do next, here are some things to try:

1. Type a few characters on the keyboard. If the program is ready to edit text, you will see the characters in the document window.

2. Browse through the menus looking for a command that starts with the word New. This command should get some action.

3. Look for a tools palette. Click on a tool, move the pointer into the document window, and click and drag the tool around the page. If there is no tools palette, but there is a Window menu, pull down that menu to see whether there is a Tools palette that can be shown.

4. Look to the File menu for unusual commands that lead to dialog boxes. Programs that rely on existing documents (such as desktop publishing programs) may have special menu items that let you bring in a document for further manipulation. For example, PageMaker's File menu offers a Place command.

5. The last resort is to go to the program's manual. We'll have more to say about that later.

Document Window Elements

All the elements we've learned about windows in the Program Manager and File Manager—title bar, control menu, minimize button, maximize button, scroll bars—can appear in document windows (see fig. 12.6). Their behavior is identical to window elements we've already seen. Don't be surprised, however, if one or more elements is missing if they don't apply to the particular kind of document you're working on.

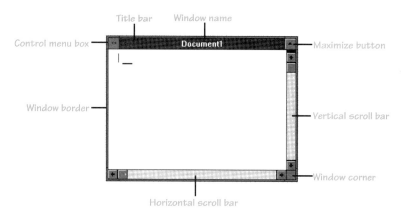

Figure 12.6
Document windows typically have the same elements as other windows we've seen.

You may, however, see additional elements. These vary from program to program, although each software publisher tends to reuse several elements to help make their products appear to be in the same family.

Closing Document Windows

Double-clicking the control menu box (or choosing Close from that control menu) closes the active window. Most programs are smart enough to know when we've made any changes to the content of a window and will ask us whether changes should be saved before the window closes. The dialog box may look something like figure 12.7.

Figure 12.7
If the file needs saving, you'll be prompted to save the changes.

Read this alert carefully and be sure to understand the impact of each button choice. The Yes button lets us store the document to the hard disk (which we'll discuss fully in the next lesson). The Cancel button is also safe, because it cancels the window closing process. It lets us take back the Close Window command.

By far the most dangerous button is the No one, because it closes the window and blows away anything we've done since the last time we saved the document (which may have been never, if we just started with a blank document window).

Mix and Maxing

When a document window maximizes, some potentially confusing things happen. Typically, the document and application windows essentially merge into one window (see fig. 12.8). The title bar assumes the name of both the program and document. As we resize the program window, so do we resize the document window with it.

Figure 12.8

A document window before (A) and after (B) maximizing. The application document windows merge.

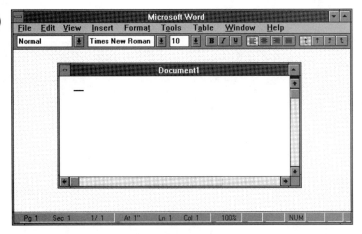

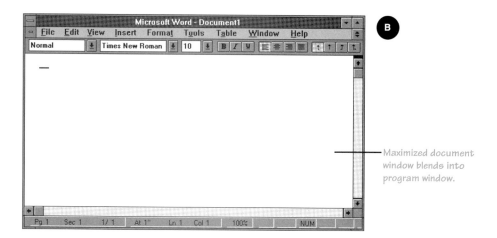

Maximized document window blends into program window.

What can be confusing is the array of minimize, maximize, and restore buttons at the top right corner of the window (see fig. 12.9). The top two govern the entire window. When we click the top right maximize button, the entire window (program and document combined) fills the screen. This position tends to give us the maximum document screen real estate—especially handy for spreadsheet and graphic documents.

Application window minimize button

Application window maximize button

Document window restore button

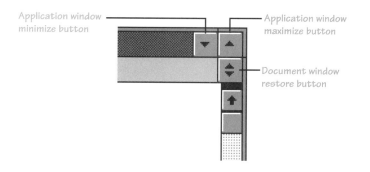

Figure 12.9
With a maximized document window, the sizing buttons get confusing.

When we minimize the entire window, not only does the program shrink to its expected icon on the desktop, but its label includes the document name—the name from the window's title bar (see fig. 12.10). This doesn't prevent us from restoring the window and opening other documents.

Figure 12.10
*A minimized combo
window reveals the
document name, too.*

The third button of this grouping pertains just to the document window
part of this conglomeration. A click of this button in its two-arrowed restore
form makes the document window a separate entity within the program
window again.

Notice, too, that in its maximized form, a document window also has its
own control menu button below the program window's control menu
button—another potential point of confusion (see fig. 12.11). Double-
clicking the lower button closes the document window; double-clicking the
top button exits the program. That's a big difference, but graphically, the
difference may not be clear until you work with this combination for some
time.

Figure 12.11
*The control menu
boxes for the merged
windows.*

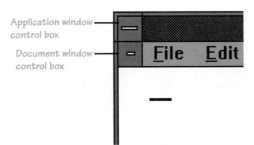

Multiple Documents

Most programs allow us to open more than one document window at a
time to facilitate flipping between documents or copying a chunk from one
to another. If a document window is separate from the application window,
the program usually allows multiple document windows. The maximum

number of windows allowed by the program usually depends on the amount of memory your program occupies and how memory-hungry each document is.

Like everything else in Windows, however, only one document window is active at any given moment. The active document window is the one on top of the pile and whose title bar is in color.

They're Out To Get Us

Although palettes and toolbars are supposedly there to help us work with a program, some programs really overdo a good thing. The result is a confusing array of incomprehensible icons and a series of small windows that do more obstructing than helping.

Although documents and other windows share lots of good things, the same cautions apply, as well. Smaller windows can be completely obscured by activating larger windows. Typically, a Window menu provides a list of all open windows within an application, and we can choose the one we want to become active (see fig. 12.12). In absence of such a menu, it may be necessary to resize or to drag the larger window to reveal the smaller one.

Figure 12.12

The Window menu helps us activate the window we want.

Check mark signals the active window.

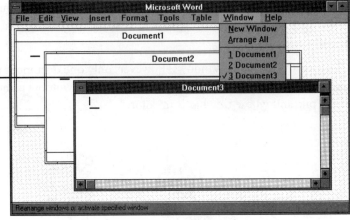

Practice

Document Window Calisthenics

1. Because I don't know which application programs are installed on your PC, we'll use the File Manager for these practice sessions, because it creates document windows just like applications do. Open the File Manager and resize the program's window as shown in figure 12.13.

Figure 12.13

The starting place for the calisthenics.

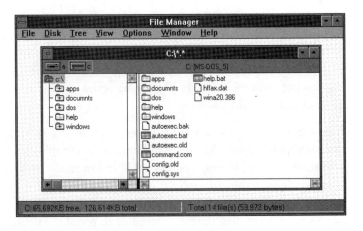

2. Click the maximize button in the directory window (analogous to a document window). Notice how the window zooms to fill the application window and observe the clusters of buttons at the upper left and right corners. The title bar includes the name of the directory (document) window.

3. Click the application window's minimize button. Notice that the desktop icon is named not only for the File Manager but also for the directory (document) window that occupies the File Manager's window.

4. Double-click the File Manager icon on the desktop to restore the window to its previous size.

5. Click the document window's restore button. The window returns to its previous size, floating freely in the program window.

6. Drag the directory (document) window around the screen with its title bar. The directory window does not go outside the program window.

Entering Information

1. Open Write.

2. Type a long sentence, such as the time-worn favorite: Now is the time for all good men to come to the aid of their country.

3. Type the sentence again in the same line. If you pause while typing (and the window is narrow enough), the document automatically scrolls so that you can see the characters you're typing. At the right margin, the text wraps to the next line without you having to type a carriage return.

4. Resize the window as shown in figure 12.14. Although you cannot see margin or tab settings, Write provides these features via dialog boxes that can be reached from menu commands. All of this behavior is a part of Write—other programs are free to do things differently (and they do).

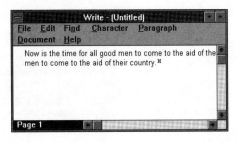

Figure 12.14
*Write and our
practice sentences.*

Closing the Document

1. Double-click the control box in the upper left corner of the window.

2. Read the dialog box shown in figure 12.15 carefully, thinking through what results from a click of each button.

Figure 12.15
Read carefully.

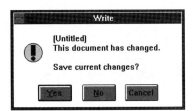

3. Click the No button, because we will create a document in the next encounter.

Summary

We've finally seen what it's like to begin working inside a program, where we perform our real work. Document windows are where all the action takes place, even if there are some ancillary palettes or toolbars on the screen. If we get by the scary part of doing some work in a window, we've learned that a program warns us to save our work before it allows us to close the window.

Exorcises

1. How can you identify whether a program can have more than one document window open at a time?

2. When multiple windows are allowed, how many can you have open at one time?

3. Identify the items in figure 12.16:

   a. program's maximize button

   b. program's minimize button

   c. document's restore button

   d. document's control menu box

   e. program's control menu box

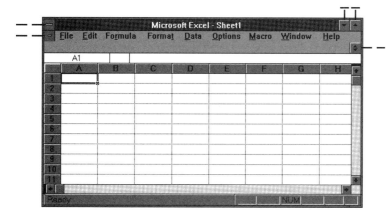

Figure 12.16
A combination application and maximized document window.

4. In figure 12.16, where would you double-click to close the document?

5. In figure 12.16 what happens when you click the minimize button?

6. A friend asks your help getting started with a new program you don't recognize on the screen. What would you do to find out what the program does and how you start using it?

Storing and Sharing Your Work

Goal

Master the methods of saving a document in the folder of your choice so that you can organize documents while you work on them.

What You Will Need

The PC turned on, Windows Write open (as we left it at the end of the 12th Encounter), at least one blank floppy disk, and one floppy disk that may have files on it.

Terms of Enfearment

Save As	SneakerNet
Save	backup
Save As dialog	floppy disk
pop-up menu	formatting
list box	double sided
default	high density
eject	

Briefing

Filing Stuff Away

In the real world, when you finish working with a document, you usually need to put it back into the folder and filing cabinet for safekeeping. Leaving it on your desk makes it vulnerable to being lost or accidentally destroyed in a spilled coffee cup catastrophe. The same is true for computer documents, but the need to put them away safely is magnified, because unlike the real world, a power outage can wipe out your last hour's work instead of just leaving you in the dark.

Storing documents to the hard disk is called *saving* a document. The longer you have a document open in a program and the more changes you make to it, the more important it becomes to save that document periodically. Saving is a way to put away a snapshot of a document at any given moment—not just when you're finished with it.

Storage Commands

Except for the handful of programs that automatically save changes as we make them (like the File Manager does when we rename a folder), all programs have both *Save As* and *Save* commands in their File menus.

Save As...

I discuss the Save As command first, because it's the one you must issue the first time you store a document (if the program lets you choose Save for a new document, it actually reacts as though you had chosen the Save As command anyway). This command leads you to the *Save As dialog* box, a feature-filled window if there ever was one (see fig. 13.1).

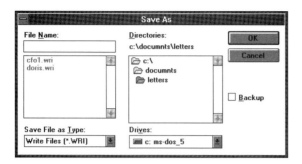

Figure 13.1
*A typical Save As
dialog box.*

In addition to letting us assign a name to the document (an absolute require-
ment for any document), the Save As dialog also lets us determine exactly
where the document should be stored. We don't have to go out to the File
Manager to move stuff around. Figure 13.1 shows a generic Save As dialog.
Some programs modify this dialog, but the basic elements are always there,
even if in a slightly different layout.

Where Are We?

Whenever you see a Save As dialog, it's important to determine which drive
and folder Windows is currently pointing to. The first place to look is the
selected drive shown in the Drives field at the bottom center of the dialog. If
we have only one hard disk volume on your system, this item will change
only if we've saved a file to a floppy disk. But, if we want or need to change
the drive, we have to use the *pop-up menu* in this location (see fig. 13.2).

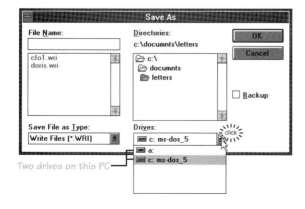

Two drives on this PC

Figure 13.2
*The Drives pop-up
menu is the first
place to look to make
sure that we're
saving to the desired
disk drive.*

These pop-up menus—denoted by the down arrow to their right—are easy to use and are common elements in dialog boxes in general. They behave like drop-down menus in a menu bar, but it's clicking on the field or arrow that makes the menu pop up (or down, as the case may be). Moreover, these menus tend to be smaller than menu bar menus, so clicking and dragging to a selection is often not practical. It's usually best to pop these guys open, scroll if necessary, and then click on the selection of your choice (see fig. 13.3).

Figure 13.3
Click the down arrow to pop the menu, scroll down, and then click on your choice.

Navigating Hard Disk Waters

After we've made sure that we're talking to the desired drive, it's time to select the desired folder (directory). The large, right-hand scrollable field (called a *list box*) presents a tree-like diagram of selected folders. If we're not sure where we are, it's best to double-click the c:\ folder, which takes us to the root view of the drive (see fig. 13.4). Then double-click the folders as if working our way through the tree diagram of the File Manager. The opened folder icon is the currently selected folder.

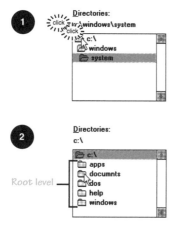

Figure 13.4
Double-click the root folder for the most global view. Then double-click your way into nested folders.

You're My Type

Here we go with file name extensions again. A lot of DOS and most Windows programs assign what they hope is a unique three-character extension to document files they create. There is method to this madness. For one, it makes it easier to recognize a file created with a particular program when viewing a file listing.

The pop-up menu of file types presented in a Save As dialog allows us to save a file from the program in any format that the program supports. For example, graphics programs may allow for different popular formats compatible with other graphics programs. The same goes for word processing or spreadsheet files, which may be saved in formats that can be easily read by other similar programs in Windows or even other computers (like the Macintosh).

It's Default of De Program

File types are, therefore, known to us by their extension (there's much more to this on the inside of the file, but only programmers worry about that). When we choose Save As for the first time in a document, the program suggests its own native file type and extension. This is called the *default*—a common computer term referring to any setting that the computer selects without any help from the user.

Up in the File Name field, the program usually pre-enters a wildcard file name for us with the extension shown in the Save File As Type field. The list box on the left then displays a list of existing files of that type in the selected folder—so we don't try to use a name that's already taken (see fig. 13.5).

Figure 13.5

The list box shows existing files of the same type in the current folder.

Dimmed names already taken in the selected directory.

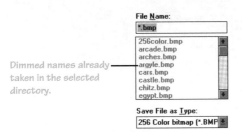

If the file is to be saved in the native format, type up to 8 characters into the File Name field—the program fills in the extension for us. The OK button may have a heavy highlighted border around it, meaning that a press of the Enter key acts the same as clicking the button.

The Old Working Directory

As you gain experience with Save As dialogs and gain comfort with your document organization, you'll see what a time and click saver the Working Directory property of Program Manager icons can be. By prespecifying a part of the destination path (e.g., c:\documnts), the directory listing in Save As dialogs is ready for just a couple of double-clicks to find a nested folder.

Subsequent Saves

After a document is saved on the hard disk, it's much easier to save later revisions. The Save command replaces the old copy with whatever state the document is in at the moment, no matter where on the hard disk the old copy came from (see fig. 13.6). To prevent lost work due to power outages, system crashes, tornadoes, and floods, issue the Save command every time you reach a point at which you don't want to lose the work you've just performed.

Figure 13.6
The Save command.

Additional Save As Uses

The Save As command comes in handy even after a document is safely stored on the disk. For example, if we want to save each revision of a document, we can't use the Save command over and over, because this command writes over any old version. When you're ready to save a new version, issue the Save As command and give the document a slightly different name (perhaps append a version number).

Saving a second copy of a document is another use for Save As. An extra copy of a file is called a *backup* and can be opened in case the original file is damaged. It is best to save a backup copy to a different drive, because severe data-losing problems tend to affect an entire disk. If another hard disk or file server is available, issue the Save As command, select the desired drive (and nested folder), and save the copy.

Working with Floppy Disks

A diskette is also called a *floppy disk*, or just floppy. Don't let the comparative sizes of the 5 1/4-inch and 3 1/2-inch disks fool you. The smaller disks represent newer technology and actually hold more information than their larger cousins.

A Really Blank Disk

For the PC to write information on a disk, the disk must be mapped out just as a parking lot has lanes and spaces painted on it (see fig. 13.7). Truly blank disks are like a freshly paved, unpainted lot. The process of setting up all those parking spaces for chunks of information is called *formatting*.

Figure 13.7
A blank disk is like an unpainted parking lot. Formatting lays out how and where information will be stored, just as parking lanes and spaces painted on the asphalt dictate how cars travel and park.

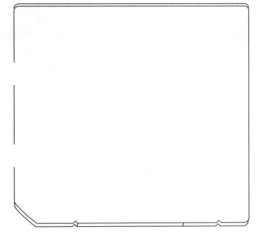

Uninitialized

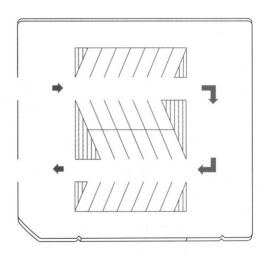

Initialized

If you're not sure that a disk is formatted, the best way to find out is to proceed with whatever you were about to do with the disk. Before Windows tries to complete the task, it checks to make sure that the disk is formatted properly (see fig. 13.8). If not, it lets us take a side trip to the formatting window (which we can also reach directly by choosing Format from the File Manager's Disk menu). Choices available to us depend on the storage capacity of the diskette we've inserted.

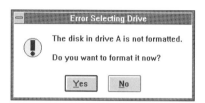

Figure 13.8

If you try to read or write to an unformatted disk, you receive a message to that effect, plus a chance to format the disk.

Disk Capacities (5 1/4-Inch)

Floppy disks of the 5 1/4-inch type come in two styles and capacities:

Double Density (DD)	360K
High Density (HD)	1.2MB

Older PCs (in fact, they would be so old and slow that you couldn't use Windows on them) may not be equipped with a disk drive capable of reading or writing to high-density diskettes, so the 360K double-density style is the most common (and the disk size on which a lot of software programs arrive).

Disk Capacities (3 1/2-Inch)

Floppy disks of the 3 1/2-inch type come in two styles and capacities:

Double Density (DD)	720K
High Density (HD)	1.4MB

The 3 1/2-inch disk drive is more recent but is quickly becoming the standard, because the disks are more durable, smaller, and capable of storing slightly more information than the high-density 5 1/4-inch disks.

High-density 3 1/2-inch disks are immediately recognizable when we look at the diskette. In addition to typical "HD" markings on the top side, an extra square hole appears in one of the corners (other than the locking tab corner). Disk drives sense when this hole is present and signal to the computer that the disk in the drive is a high-density one.

What's on the Disk

To the File Manager, a floppy disk is just a small volume, like a tiny hard disk. We can double-click the drive icon at the top of the File Manager window to open a window showing the directory of a floppy (see fig. 13.9). On the disk may be icons of the same varieties we see on the hard disk.

Figure 13.9
*A floppy disk
directory window.*

Selected floppy drive

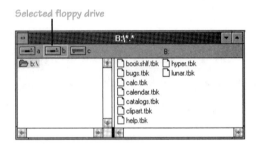

Ejecting the Disk

To remove a floppy, the process depends on whether the disk is 5 1/4-inch or 3 1/2-inch, because each size drive handles disks differently. For the 5 1/4-inch disk, flip the latch in front of the drive and slowly pull out the disk. A 3 1/2-inch drive is more deeply seated in the drive, so it needs a push. We start by firmly pressing the button above the disk slit. This action *ejects* the disk from the grasp of the mechanism, and we can pull it slowly the rest of the way.

Copying a File to a Floppy

The point of this encounter was to show you how to copy a file to a floppy disk to share with another PC user. To do so, you don't even have to open a File Manager window for the floppy. Instead, drag one or more files (or folders) from the listing in the hard disk window to the floppy disk drive's icon (usually the A drive) as shown in figure 13.10. After one or more confirmation dialogs, a progress dialog lets us know how the copying is going.

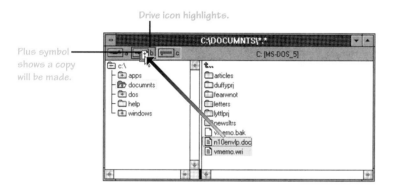

Figure 13.10
Dragging selected files to the floppy drive.

If we're trying to jam more stuff onto the diskette than it has room for, the File Manager alerts us as soon as the destination disk is full (see fig. 13.11). The alert dialog lets us continue the copy to another diskette—just remove the one that's in there and insert another.

Figure 13.11
When the floppy fills up, we can continue on another.

When we're done, we can put on our sneakers and speed our way to the colleague who needs the files—via *SneakerNet.*

Floppies as Backup

It's vital that we keep extra copies of documents someplace other than the hard disk where they are normally stored. If something dreadful should happen to the hard disk, we at least have a recent copy of important data.

Copying changed documents to floppy disks is one way to perform this backup operation. A number of commercial backup utility programs facilitate the process. Remember, however, that a full 80 MB hard disk could require as many as 58 high-density floppy disks for a complete backup—but far fewer just for your documents.

Floppy Copying

We've seen how to copy some files to a floppy. But, if we want to make an additional copy of that floppy disk, we use the File Manager for that as well.

To start the process, choose Copy Disk from the Disk menu. Alert dialog messages instruct us to first insert the disk we want to copy. Windows reads a copy of the disk into memory temporarily. Then it asks for us to switch floppies and to put the destination disk in the drive (see fig. 13.12). At that point, the memory copy of the disk is written to the destination. When the disk copying is completed, the destination disk contains the exact contents of the original.

Figure 13.12

Copying one disk to another.

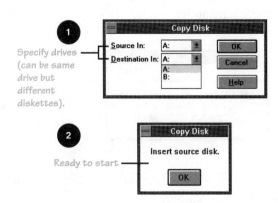

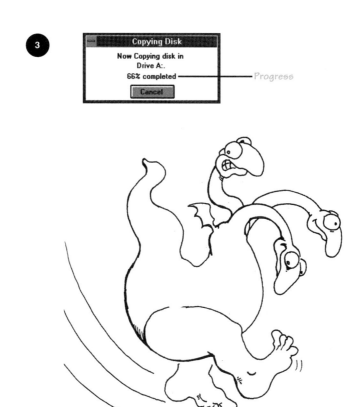

They're Out To Get Us

One of the biggest confusions for new Windows users is losing files—not eternally lost, just in some unknown place on the hard disk. If you forget to specify the location in a Save As dialog box, you can always use the File Manager's Search command to locate a file by name (or partial name with wildcard characters).

If you feel that you're getting lost while navigating through folders via the Save As directory list, double-click the c:\ folder and take it from the top.

Even from the Save As dialog, Windows won't let you overwrite an existing file with the same name within a folder. An alert asks that you confirm your desire to replace an old file with that name.

Although Windows warns you about anything that will lose information, it can't save you from yourself. Closing a changed window without saving the document (clicking "No") will lose those changes forever. Welcome to personal computing.

The thorniest potential problem is that when you remove a diskette from the drive, the File Manager window showing that disk's directory doesn't know any better. As far as the File Manager is concerned, the original diskette is still there, even if you insert something else. That means that the directory in the File Manager window may not be accurate. The simplest way to make sure that the window reflects reality after inserting a disk is to click that drive's icon in the window. This action is the same as issuing the Refresh command in the Window menu.

Another possible confusion inducer is the different effect of clicking and double-clicking on a drive icon in a File Manager window. Here's a quick way to understand the difference:

Click Type	Action
Single	Shows drive's contents in *current* window
Double	Shows drive's contents in a *new* window

Accidentally clicking a drive changes the directory window to another drive unexpectedly; double-clicking a drive by accident opens another window, even if that directory already has a window in the File Manager. The simplest method is to leave a directory window to any hard disk or file server (networked hard disk) open (tile or cascade as you prefer); open floppy disk directories only when you're copying stuff to-and-fro.

Another quizzical event is when a diskette initialization fails (a dialog tells you so). If, after a second try, initialization still fails, it usually means that the disk has gone bad. Toss it in the trash.

Practice

Saving a Document the First Time

1. While in Write, choose New from the File menu.

2. Type the memo as shown in figure 13.13.

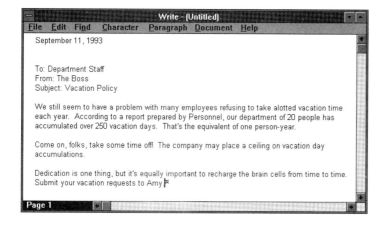

Figure 13.13
A sample memo we'll use a lot.

3. Choose Save As.

4. Type the name of the document as *vmemo*, **but don't press Enter.**

5. If it's not set so, change the current folder to the Documnts folder by doing the following:

   a. double-clicking the c:\ folder in the directory listing on the right;

   b. double-clicking the Documnts folder.

6. Click the OK button. This stores the file on the hard disk.

Look for File

1. Open (or switch to) the File Manager.

2. Click the root folder.

3. Choose Search from the File menu, type *vmemo**, and press Return. The File Manager should locate your new file.

Subsequent Save

1. Switch back to Write.

2. Add a line of text to the last paragraph of the document.

3. Pull down the File menu and issue the Save command. Write saves the new version.

Saving a Backup

1. Choose Save As from the File menu. Notice that the default settings still point to the Documnts folder.

2. Enter *vmemo.bak* as the file name, **but don't press Enter.** The bak extension is commonly used as meaning a backup copy.

3. Double-click the c:\ folder.

4. Click the OK button to save this backup copy to the root directory.

5. Notice that the name of the document window has changed to the backup (see fig. 13.14). Choose Save As and see that the default settings point to the root folder—the last place the document was saved.

6. Click the Cancel button.

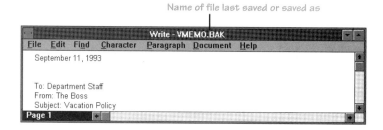

Name of file last saved or saved as

Figure 13.14
*After the Save As
command, the active
window changes to
the most recently
saved name.*

Format a Disk

1. Open the File Manager.

2. Insert a blank (or empty) high-density disk into the diskette drive. Nothing happens in the File Manager to indicate that anything is different.

3. Choose Format Disk from the Disk menu. Use the pop-up menus in the Format dialog box to select the disk drive letter (usually A) and the highest capacity setting for the type of disk drive.

4. Press the Tab key until the text pointer is in the Label field. Type *Backup1* (no spaces) as the disk's name. Disk labels are rarely used but will help us identify this diskette for the rest of this Practice session.

5. Double-click the floppy drive's icon in any open File Manager directory window. Another window opens, showing the emptiness that is Backup1. Note at the very bottom of the File Manager window the amount of space already occupied and how much is available.

Copying to a Disk

1. Locate the *VMemo* file in the hard disk directory and drag it to the floppy disk drive's icon (see fig. 13.15). Agree to any confirmation alerts.

Figure 13.15

*Dragging a file to
the floppy icon.*

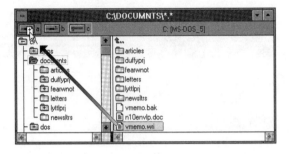

2. If the A:\ directory window has been obscured, pull down the Window menu and choose the A:\ window. Otherwise, double-click the A drive icon to open a directory window for the drive.

Summary

For most programs, we must specifically save our work in progress to the hard disk for it to be safe. The Save As dialog lets us give a new document its name and navigate to a location on the hard disk for us to save the document. Save As lets us name and locate a document, and the plain Save command updates the existing file with a copy of our work at the moment. We should issue the Save command each time we want to preserve the latest effort that went into a document.

We've learned quite a lot about floppy disks, including how to lock, insert, and remove them. Copying files to or from a diskette is the same process as copying files to or from any drive in the File Manager.

Exorcises

1. In which menu are commands for saving files?

2. Explain the differences between the actions of the Save and Save As commands.

3. You can store documents at the c:\ root folder: True or False?

4. If you choose Save while viewing an untitled, unsaved document, what will happen on the screen?

5. How often should you save a document while you're working on it?

6. Is it possible to save a new document to a floppy disk instead of the hard disk?

7. If you are viewing the File Manager and have a directory window open for a floppy disk, what should you do whenever you change diskettes?

8. How do you erase an individual file from a diskette? How do you erase the diskette?

Exiting, Resting, and Restarting a Program

Goal

Learn how to exit (quit) and restart a program in your sleep, as well as learn productive methods for temporarily putting away programs you use a lot.

What You Will Need

PC turned on, Windows Write running, and the document created in the 13th Encounter open.

Terms of Enfearment

exit
associate
Ctrl+Alt+Del

Briefing

Why Are You Quitting?

There are two reasons why you would want to close down—*exit*—
a program:

- You're about to shut down the PC.

- You need to make memory available to load another program.

Before shutting down your PC, you should close down all programs that are
running (except for the DOS, which always runs while the PC is on). It's
not vital to exit Windows before switching off the PC, but it's a good idea:
when you shut down Windows, it commands all programs to quit before it
does. This process may discover that a program contains a document you
have changed but have not yet stored on the hard disk.

If your machine is running low on available RAM, exiting a program also
makes memory available for starting other programs (usually, that is—see
the 20th Encounter).

Adios!

In the control menu of all application windows is either a Close or Exit
command. Additionally, some programs contain an Exit command in their
File menus. Double-clicking the control menu box is still a friendly, consis-
tent way of exiting any program.

When we exit a program that has open document windows, the program
first checks whether any of those documents need saving because changes
have been made to the documents. If so, we see the same dialog box that we
get when closing a window of a changed document (see fig. 14.1). This
dialog box, which lets us save or discard the changes, appears for each
document that might need saving.

Figure 14.1
*We're given a chance
to save changed
documents.*

Restarting a Program

You saw a couple ways to start an application in the 11th Encounter. Those methods apply here to get an application running again. But, there is also one nifty speedcut.

The Windows File Manager allows us to *associate* document files with a particular application. There isn't all that much magic involved here, because the association is based solely on the three-letter file name extension. For example, if we associate the doc extension with Microsoft Word for Windows, a couple of things happen. First, any File Manager document icon with a file name extension that has been associated to a program takes on a slightly different look—the little lines appear in the icon (see fig. 14.2). Visually, it doesn't tell us which program is associated with the file, but we know there is some connection.

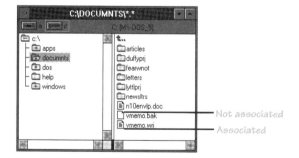

Figure 14.2
*Associated file icons
have the little lines in
them.*

Secondly, we can double-click the icon to start the program and load the document—all ready for us to go. Unfortunately, we cannot open multiple documents from the File Manager in this way.

The Association

Establishing an association is a painless task in the File Manager. Click once on a file whose extension you recognize to be unique to the program that generated the file. Choose Associate from the File menu. In the succeeding dialog box shown in figure 14.3, ignore everything except the Browse button. Click that button to see a file dialog box.

Figure 14.3

Associating an extension to an application.

The File Manager sets up the dialog so that only program files (or files that trigger programs) are listed in the left pane. Double-click the c:\ folder to start navigating through the rest of the folders in search of the program file (usually a file ending in exe). Select the program file and click OK. Until you change the association, *all files with that extension* (on any disk) are associated with that program.

Minimize versus Exit

It can be a nasty habit to double-click a program's control menu box when you're finished with the program. When you need the program later, you have to locate the icon in the Program Manager or File Manager and wait for the program to load. A better habit to instill in your routine is to head for the program's minimize button, rather than the control menu box.

A click of the minimize button keeps the program running but reduces it to an icon at the bottom of the Windows desktop. A double-click restores the window to its previous glory, without making you wait for the program to load (see fig. 14.4). Therefore, minimize during the day and choose the desired program from an iconic "menu" at the bottom of the desktop. Save exiting for times when you need the memory for other processes or when you're shutting down for the day.

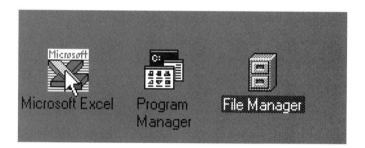

Figure 14.4
Minimized programs ready at a double-click.

They're Out To Get Us

Sometimes, for no apparent reason (but for probable reasons outlined in the 19th Encounter), a program may lock up on you—the pointer may react to the mouse, but nothing you click on does anything. A *freeze* is also known as a *hang*, which is usually what you want to do to yourself if you haven't saved your work recently. When this happens, try the following steps in order:

1. Press the Escape key. Some programs might be in an endless loop, which this keyboard command can break.

2. Hold down the Control, Alt, and Delete keys (*Ctrl+Alt+Del*). This key sequence normally restarts the computer. Windows, however, traps this command before it gets all the way to your PC's hardware. You'll see a message that lets you quit the current program without disturbing others that are running (and may have unsaved work open). Press any single key to exit the one program. If nothing happens, proceed to step 3; otherwise, save all the work in other applications, quit them, exit Windows, and restart your PC by pressing Ctrl+Alt+Del again.

3. Look for a rear panel push-button labeled *Reset*. This feature is common in laptop PCs but not on desktop models. If your PC has such a button and if you press it, the machine should restart. If it still doesn't, go to the last step.

4. Turn off the PC via its power button or switch. This is the last resort but will certainly get you out of any jam.

Missing Associations

Although opening an application by double-clicking one of its documents is neat, it may not work if the application that created the file is not on your hard disk (see fig. 14.5). This can easily happen if someone gives you a file from another machine that contains other types of programs. Or, you may

have removed an associated application from your hard disk. If you know
what kind of file it is (for example, word processing, graphics), you may be
able to open the file from within a similar kind of application. Many
programs can open and convert files from other formats.

Figure 14.5

*An alert warns you if
the associated
application can't be
found—it may be in
another folder or not
on your disk at all.*

Extra Associations

One final annoyance has to do with the fact that file name extensions are not
always unique. It's not uncommon, for example, for different DOS programs' Help systems to have files bearing the hlp extension. That also
happens to be the extension for Windows and Windows applications help
files. Files ending in hlp are associated with a program (winhelp.exe) that
provides a common on-line help face for everything in Windows. The
problem is that winhelp.exe requires that its hlp files have an internal
structure that works only with that program. A DOS program's hlp file
won't work with winhelp.exe—and an alert message tells you that if you
double-click a non-Windows help file in the File Manager (see fig. 14.6).

Figure 14.6

*A file with an
extension associated
with one program
may actually belong
to another program.
Launching by
association won't
work in this case.*

If you encounter a problem like this and need to access a file with a program other than the one with which it is associated, open the program first and then open the document (I cover this topic in the next Encounter).

Practice

Exiting

1. Open the Note Pad accessory program. Pull down the File menu and notice the Exit command—but do not choose it now.

2. Type a few words into the Note Pad window.

3. Double-click the control menu box (the same as choosing Exit from the File menu in this program). Read the fail-safe dialog about the note you just typed (see fig. 14.7). Click Yes.

Figure 14.7

An alert about saving changes.

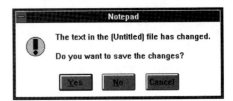

Restarting a Program

1. In the File Manager, locate the original Vacation Memo file. It has a wri extension, the extension assigned by the Write program.

2. Select the icon and choose Associate from the File menu. In the Associate dialog box that appears, notice that wri files are associated with Write. Close the Associate window.

3. Double-click the Vacation Memo file icon. Write loads, and the memo appears.

Minimizing

1. Click the minimize button in the Write window to shrink this program to a desktop icon.

2. Open the Calculator accessory and click the minimize button to shrink
   this program to a desktop icon.

3. Double-click each program and minimize it again. Repeat this step five
   times or until you feel that you don't have to think about reaching for
   the minimize button to put a program away for the time being.

Summary

We've learned the universal way to exit any Windows application and that
we should minimize programs. The File Manager lets us associate files with
specific extensions, so we can re-open a document and its application by
double-clicking the document icon.

Exorcises

1. By what names are the commands to quit Windows applications
   known? Where are those commands available for our mouse?

2. In figure 14.8, describe the results of clicking each of the buttons.

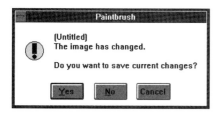

Figure 14.8
*What does each
button do?*

WARNING!
QUICKSAND

Working with an Existing Document

Goal

Start using basic text-editing techniques, while learning how to shuffle text and pictures from document to document or program to program.

What You Will Need

PC turned on and Windows running with all applications closed.

Terms of Enfearment

Open dialog	Copy
text insertion pointer	Paste
text cursor	Undo
font	Clipboard Viewer
Clipboard	draw objects
Cut	bitmaps

Briefing

Opening a Document

We've already learned how to open a document from the File Manager by double-clicking it. But, when we're already inside a program, we can open a document without switching to the File Manager. All document-oriented programs provide an Open command in the File menu (see fig. 15.1).

Figure 15.1
*The Open
command.*

This ellipsis-toting command leads to an *Open dialog* box, a simpler cousin of the Save As dialog we've already met (see fig. 15.2). In fact, because we know how to use the Save As dialog, we already know everything there is to know about the Open dialog: how to navigate through volumes and folders to locate a file. The only difference in behavior is that file names are not dimmed in the file list. To open a file, we select it and click the OK button—or better yet, double-click on the file name.

Figure 15.2
*The Open dialog
box. Navigate to
the desired folder and
then double-click
the file.*

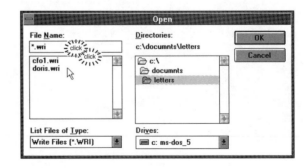

You may use the List Files of Type pop-up menu shown in figure 15.3 more often in the Open dialog, because it lets you view names of documents in other formats (they'll have file name extensions other than the one generated by the program). For example, you may want to use your word processing program to view a plain text file (saved that way by someone else in her word processing program). By listing files with the txt extension, you will more likely see that file listed in some folder on your hard disk.

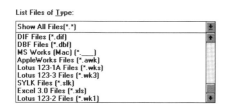

Figure 15.3
One program's extensive file type list indicates that it can accommodate files from many formats and other programs.

Typing Text

Unless your work is entirely graphical, a lot of what you do on the PC is entering and editing text in documents. We had a taste of this in creating the vacation memo in the 13th Encounter. As we typed, the *text insertion pointer*—the flashing vertical line in a document—pointed to where the next character we typed would go. This insertion pointer is independent of the mouse pointer.

Positioning the Pointer

We do, however, use the mouse pointer to reposition the text insertion pointer within a chunk of text. Whenever the mouse pointer rolls atop an editable area, the pointer changes its appearance from the arrow to a *text cursor*. The text cursor is one pixel wide for a reason: it lets us position it *between* characters in a line of text. If we then click the mouse button, the flashing text insertion pointer appears in that spot. The next characters we type insert themselves starting at that location, pushing the text after it to the right and down. Windows text never overwrites other text (unless that other text is selected, below).

Short Moves

If we need to move the text insertion pointer only a few characters or lines, it may be more convenient to use the four arrow keys on the keyboard. A press of each of these keys moves the text insertion pointer one unit (character or line) in the direction of the arrow. Some programs enhance this motion if we hold down a modifier key, such as the Control key, to do things like jump forward or back by a full word, rather than by one character.

Selecting Text

Much of Windows operation consists of a sequence of the following:

- Selecting something
- Issuing a command that affects the selected item

The same is true for working with text. We first must select a range of characters—from a single character to the entire document, if necessary—and then issue a command.

We use the mouse pointer to select text in a three-step series as shown in figure 15.4:

1. Position the mouse pointer (in its text cursor shape) to the left of the character where the selection begins.

2. Click and drag the pointer until it is located to the right of the last character of the selection. As you drag, the area becomes highlighted.

3. Release the mouse button.

Figure 15.4

Selecting a chunk of text.

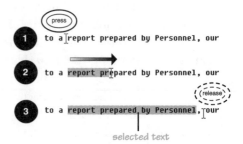

When text is selected, we can make menu choices that affect the selection, such as changing the *font* style to boldface. The selection persists, so we can perform additional actions on the same selection (for example, increasing the size of the characters). A click anywhere else deselects the text.

Selection Speedcuts

Common to all Windows text editing are a couple of speedcuts to make work life a bit easier. The most important is a double-click on a word to select the entire word (see fig. 15.5). Text-intensive programs usually have additional, non-standard speedcuts such as this to select entire lines or paragraphs.

Entire word is selected

Figure 15.5
Double-click anywhere on a word to select it.

Another useful speedcut helps select a large chunk of text even if it extends down several scrollings of a document window. The steps are as follows:

1. Position the text insertion pointer and click at the beginning of the intended selection.

2. If necessary, *without clicking again in the document*, scroll down until the end of the selection is in view.

3. Hold down the Shift key and click at the end of the intended selection (see fig. 15.6).

The entire range is instantly selected, and any action we perform works on the entire range, even if not all of it is in view.

We still seem to have a problem with many employees refusing
to take alotted vacation time each year. According to a
report prepared by Personnel, our department of 20 people has
accumulated over 250 vacation days. That's the equivalent of
one person-year.

Figure 15.6

Shift-selecting a large chunk of text.

We still seem to have a problem with many employees refusing
to take alotted vacation time each year. According to a
report prepared by Personnel, our department of 20 people has
accumulated over 250 vacation days. That's the equivalent of
one person-year.

⇧Shift + click

Moving Text Around

Built into Windows is a most convenient facility called the *Clipboard*—a temporary storage space for anything we can select in a document. When something is stored in the Clipboard, we can take it to another place in the document, to another document, even to another program.

To get something into the Clipboard, we first select it. Then we issue one of two commands in the Edit menu: *Copy* or *Cut.* Copy places an exact copy of the selected information into the Clipboard, leaving the original intact (see fig. 15.7); Cut removes the original after copying it to the Clipboard (see fig. 15.8).

Figure 15.7

Copying places the selected information into a special place in memory called the Clipboard.

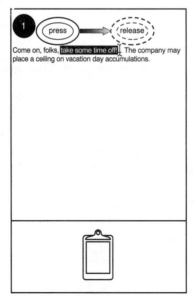

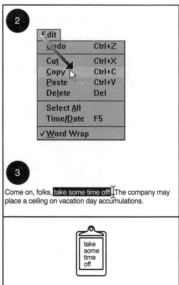

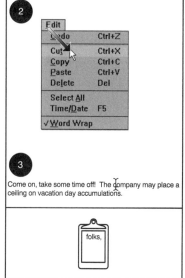

Figure 15.8

Cutting removes selected information and keeps a copy in the Clipboard. The Clipboard holds only the most recently copied or cut data.

To get something out of the Clipboard and into a document, we issue the *Paste* command. To paste text, however, we first must indicate where we want it to go by positioning the flashing text insertion pointer at the desired location. The Paste command then inserts the data from the Clipboard into the document (see fig. 15.9).

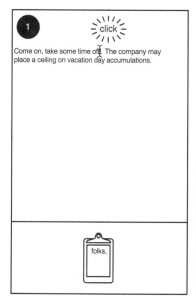

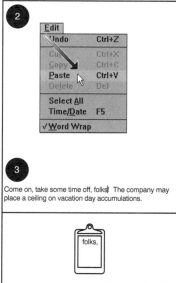

Figure 15.9

Pasting data from the Clipboard does not affect the contents of the Clipboard.

Pasting information does not remove it from the Clipboard, so we can paste the same Clipboard information in as many places as we want. Because the Clipboard can hold only one piece of information at a time, however, the next time we Copy or Cut anything, we will overwrite what was in there before. Most importantly, the Clipboard is also wiped clean when we exit Windows.

Oh No!

Just like working with scissors and glue, it is possible while cutting and pasting in a Windows program to cut the wrong stuff or paste in the wrong place. This is where Windows has one up over the real world. As long as we recognize an error right away, we can usually make everything better by choosing the *Undo* command in the Edit menu. Not all programs offer Undo, but most programs do. Issuing the Undo command after an errant Cut restores the text to its uncut state; after an errant Paste, Undo lifts the inserted text from the document.

Deleting without Cutting

We have two quicker ways to delete text that we won't need for pasting later. Both methods start with the deletable text selected. One method is as simple as pressing either the Backspace key at the upper right of the typewriter keys on the keyboard or the Delete key (see fig. 15.10). Press, poof: it's gone.

Figure 15.10

The Backspace and Delete keys erase selected information without affecting the Clipboard.

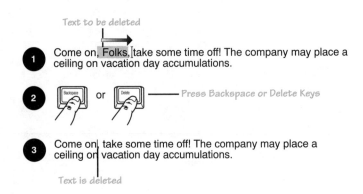

Text to be deleted

1. Come on, Folks, take some time off! The company may place a ceiling on vacation day accumulations.

2. Backspace or Delete ——— Press Backspace or Delete Keys

3. Come on, take some time off! The company may place a ceiling on vacation day accumulations.

Text is deleted

When the deleted text is actually going to be replaced by text we type or by text pasted from the Clipboard, all we have to do is select the deletable text. The next character we type or chunk we paste removes the selected text (see fig. 15.11). Well-designed programs make even these deleting actions undo-able. Thank Heaven for Undo!

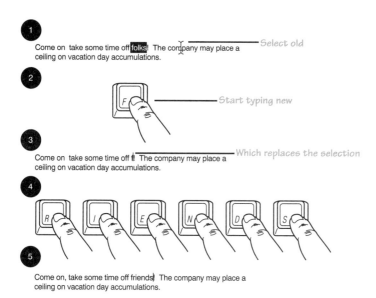

Figure 15.11
The quickest way to replace text is to select the old and then type the new.

Long-Term Clipboard: Clipboard Files

Because the Clipboard is wiped clean when we shut down Windows, it is not the best place to store frequently used tidbits—chunks of favorite text, art, sounds. But, we can use the *Clipboard Viewer* program that comes with Windows to help us out.

The Clipboard Viewer is a single-window application that displays whatever happens to be in the Windows Clipboard at the moment. It offers a short File menu, containing commands for saving the contents of the Clipboard to a file or for loading the Clipboard from an existing clipboard file (see fig. 15.12). Clipboard files are saved with the clp extension.

Figure 15.12
*The Clipboard
Viewer window and
its File menu for
saving to disk.*

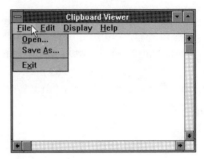

Although this isn't necessarily the easiest design for maintaining a library of
frequently used document pieces—boilerplate text sections, logo art, and so
on—you can use the Clipboard Viewer this way. After you open a clipboard
file, all you do is paste the contents into your document as you would with
any Clipboard item (see fig. 15.13).

Figure 15.13
*To transfer a
Clipboard file to a
document, open it
via the Clipboard
Viewer and then
paste.*

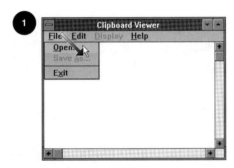

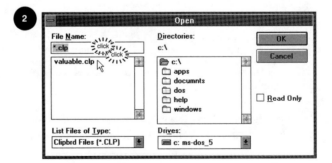

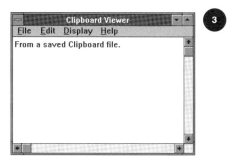

In Notepad window

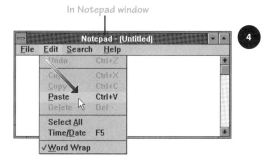

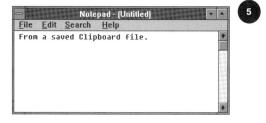

Selecting Graphics

Although we're talking about selecting, copying, and pasting stuff, we'll just touch on how to work with graphics documents. The trick is knowing how to select graphics, which depends on whether the graphics are objects (somewhat tangible items, often called *draw objects*) or just collections of pixels in the document (usually called *bitmaps*—a layout of pixels).

Graphics objects let us click on them as distinct elements of the document. A selected object displays four or more rectangles at the corners (see fig. 15.14). Such objects can be dragged, copied, or cut. These graphics are the easiest kind to work with.

Figure 15.14

This tree and sun are comprised of dozens of objects. We've selected the sun and dragged it a bit to show this component more clearly.

Selecting bitmaps is a bit trickier. It usually requires one of two tools found in the program's tools palette. Both tools let us draw an area on the screen to select, either in a freehand outline we draw (lasso tool) or in a rectangle (selection rectangle tool). After we make a selection, the outline of the area or every dark pixel within the area flickers. Specific behavior of such a selection varies from program to program, but that's one way to get art into the Scrapbook for insertion into other documents.

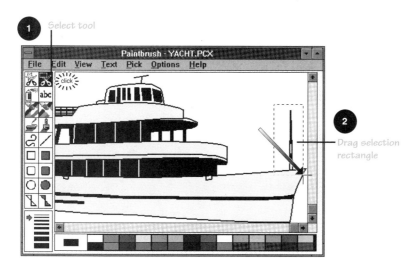

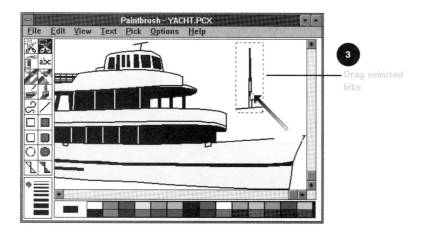

Figure 15.15

Here, we use Paintbrush's selection rectangle to select a region of pixels and then drag that region up and to the left.

They're Out To Get Us

Be angry, but don't be surprised if some egregious error you want undone doesn't undo. First of all, you usually have to catch your error right away before doing anything else that is undoable, because programs generally remember only the last undo-able thing they do. Also, sometimes programs don't support undo for every action. It never hurts to try Undo, but it will hurt when it doesn't work when you need it.

One last important gotcha here is that not all documents can accept all types of information from the Clipboard. The Note Pad, for example, does not accept graphics pasted from the Clipboard. The Paste command is dimmed when the Clipboard contains something that the program cannot handle. Programs try their best to use what they can from the Clipboard, but sometimes it's a case of comparing kiwis to kumquats.

Practice

Opening a File

1. Activate Write and choose Open from the File menu.

2. Locate the Vacation Memo file and double-click its entry in the file list.

Entering and Replacing Text

1. Position the text insertion pointer between the words *a* and *problem* in the first line of the first paragraph of the body of the memo.

2. Type *serious* and a space to add the word.

3. Double-click the word to select it.

4. Type *major* to replace the selected word.

Moving Text to Another Program

1. Select the To, From, and Subject lines only through the colon following Subject (see fig. 15.16).

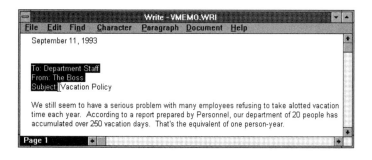

Figure 15.16
Drag-select the lines shown.

2. Choose Copy from the Edit menu. Those lines are now in the Clipboard.

3. Open the Clipboard Viewer program to view the Clipboard's contents.

4. Switch to the File Manager.

5. Switch to the Clipboard Viewer. The contents of the Clipboard survives switching between applications (see fig. 15.17).

Figure 15.17

The Clipboard Viewer shows that the contents are still there after switching between programs.

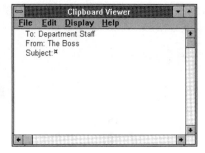

6. Open the Note Pad program.

7. Choose Paste from the Edit menu. A copy of those lines are now in the Note Pad (see fig. 15.18).

Figure 15.18

Pasting the Clipboard's contents into the Note Pad.

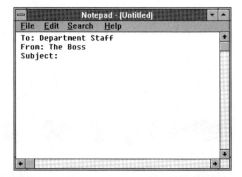

Playing with Undo

1. Insert the word "Date:" and today's date above the text (press Enter at the end of the line to shift the other lines down).

2. Choose Undo from the Edit menu. The Note Pad supports undo for typed text, so your last text entry is undone.

3. Press Control-Z (Undo) a few times to toggle between the two versions.

4. Select all the text in this Note Pad page and press the Backspace key to remove it.

5. Close the Note Pad window.

The Ephemeral Clipboard

1. Quit all programs except the Program Manager and Clipboard Viewer.

2. Use the Save command in the File menu to preserve a copy of the Clipboard's contents for a later exorcise.

3. Double-click the Program Manager's control menu box to exit Windows. This action erases the Clipboard without asking or reminding.

4. At the DOS C:\> prompt, type *win* to restart Windows.

5. When Windows is back up, open the Clipboard Viewer. It is empty upon startup.

Cut, Copy, Paste from Keyboard

1. Open the Clipboard file saved in the previous exorcise. This brings the Vacation Memo text lines into view.

2. Start Write.

3. In a blank, untitled window, type Control-V (Paste).

4. Place the text insertion pointer anywhere in the text and type Control-V again.

5. Spend several minutes cutting, copying, and pasting sections of text using the skills of selecting and issuing commands from the keyboard (Control-X, -C, and -V).

Summary

In this action-packed encounter, we've seen how to open existing documents and how to use basic text editing skills. The Clipboard is an important facility to aid in working with documents and their contents.

Exorcises

1. What are all the ways to get information into the Clipboard?

2. What are all the ways to get information out of the Clipboard into a document?

3. What is the most efficient way to replace existing text with something new from the keyboard?

4. How would you preserve the Clipboard's contents from one Windows session to another?

5. Describe the steps you would use to move an entire paragraph from one location in a document to another location in the same document.

16th Encounter

Printing a Document

Goal

To learn how to navigate through the dialog boxes required to print a document.

What You Will Need

PC turned on, with Write running and the VMemo.doc file open; a printer connected to your PC and its power switched on.

Terms of Enfearment

font	portrait (vertical) printing
TrueType	landscape (sideways) printing
PostScript	Print Manager
printer driver	background printing
Print Setup	spooling

Briefing

Know Thy Printer...

Before we can do any printing, it is vital that we know what kind of printer is connected to the PC. Each class of printer expects different signals from Windows, so we have to tell our copy of Windows which printer it will be talking to.

...and Thy Printer's Fonts

One of the biggest attractions to the graphical Windows environment is that text documents can display and easily print with a variety of typefaces. In the personal computing world, the terms *typeface* and *font*, although quite different in their true meanings, have become synonymous, and most people just use font. Personal computing fonts—especially in Windows—is a complex subject, but I'll take a stab at reducing it to a practical minimum.

Knowledge of Font

A font is a design for a set of characters, usually letters, numbers, punctuation, and other symbols we put into documents. To change the font of text in a document, select the text and then locate the menu item leading to a font dialog box as shown in figure 16.1. (This command often comes under a Format menu.) Some programs also place the list of fonts in a pop-up menu in a toolbar.

Font names that appear in the list vary depending on which printer you've selected for the current document. Some fonts are always in the list—the ones bearing the double-T icon. This icon stands for *TrueType*, a font technology that allows a given font design to be displayed on the screen and printed on any compatible printer in any size you select (the fonts are said to be scalable to any size).

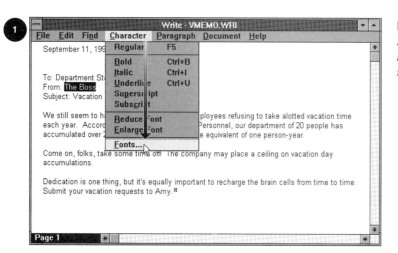

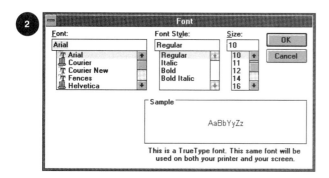

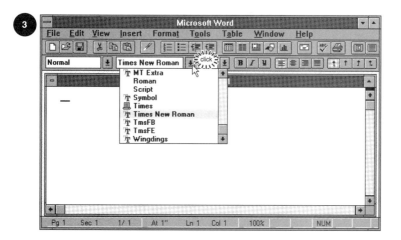

Figure 16.1
Fonts can be listed in dialog box lists or menus.

Other fonts in the list have a small printer icon before their names. These are the ones that vary from printer to printer. Sometimes, these fonts are built into the printer; other times, they are font files that get transferred to the printer when they're needed for a document. This category includes *PostScript* fonts. PostScript is another technology that defines a font's design for a printer. The on-screen presentation of a PostScript font comes either from another kind of font file, called a *screen font*, or from the PostScript font file itself (but this method requires additional software, Adobe Type Manager—ATM—to translate the font design for the screen).

One other group of fonts has no icons before its fonts names. Most of these fonts are used by Windows in its display and shouldn't be used in documents headed for the printer.

What To Use

With all that gibberish, what should you use for your documents? If the output is going to a PostScript printer (predominantly laser printers and image-setting machines at service bureaus for high-quality printing), use PostScript printer fonts exclusively. But, if your printer does not have PostScript built in, use TrueType fonts. They'll look good on the screen and print quite nicely. After all that, it's kind of simple.

You, Over There!

The first step in making Windows printable on your PC took place during the Windows installation process, during which you specified one or more printers you intended to use. That process installed *printer driver* files into the System folder inside your Windows folder. Printer drivers are files that contain instructions Windows used to control a specific type of printer.

If more than one printer driver is installed, one more step is necessary: telling Windows which printer driver to use as the default. For this step, the Printers control panel provides the necessary powers (see fig. 16.2). Click on one of the printers listed and click the Set As Default Printer button.

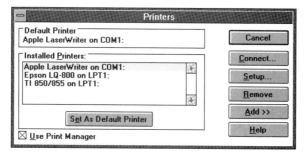

Figure 16.2
*The Printers control
panel lists all printer
drivers installed and
lets you set one to be
the default printer.*

Printing Sideways

Sometimes, documents are wider than a typical page. Spreadsheets and
graphics, especially, may be printed best with the paper sideways. Control
for this feature is most often located in a special dialog available in all
printable applications. In the File menu, in the vicinity of the Print command, is a *Print Setup* command (see fig. 16.3).

Figure 16.3
*The Print Setup
command.*

The precise contents of the Print Setup dialog varies significantly from driver
to driver, because each printer model has a specific range of settings (see
fig. 16.4). But, they all share in common a two-icon selection between
vertical (*portrait*) and sideways (*landscape*) printing. These settings also affect
the document in the document window. The virtual page on the screen
usually changes so that it is turned sideways. Therefore, it's best to make this
setting early in your work on a document. Print Setup affects only the active
document and is saved as an attribute of the document in its file. Thus, we
can choose an envelope paper size and save it with an envelope file.

Figure 16.4
*Print Setup dialogs
vary from printer to
printer, but all let us
set the page orienta-
tion.*

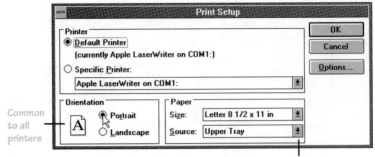

Figure 16.4
*Print Setup dialogs
vary from printer to
printer, but all let us
set the page orienta-
tion.*

Common
to all
printers

Change with selected printer

Can We Print Now?

To print a document, make sure that it is the active window in the application and choose Print from the File menu. A *Print dialog* appears, giving us
some further control over the printing (see fig. 16.5). Among the most
important optional settings are how many copies we want, if we want just a
portion of a document or all pages, and whether the paper will come from
the paper tray or from our manually feeding a special kind of paper (or
envelope).

Click the OK button, and Windows takes over.

Figure 16.5
*Each printer's Print
dialog looks slightly
different, but we can
always specify the
number of copies and
page range. Click
OK to start printing.*

For all
printers

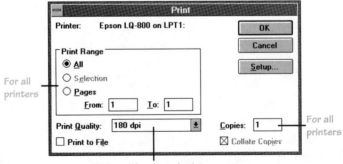

For all
printers

Varies with selected printer

One Printer, No Waiting

More precisely, it is the Windows *Print Manager* that takes over. Documents quickly "print" to an intermediate file we don't normally see. The Print Manager begins feeding printing information to the printer as quickly as the printer can accept. Because that speed is usually slower than we work, we let the Print Manager perform what is called *background printing*, while we continue working on other stuff. We don't have to wait for the complete document to reach real paper (although the computer sometimes freezes momentarily while sending signals to the printer). Background printing is also known by the name *spooling*, and the software that monitors spooling is called a *spooler*.

The Print Manager is Windows' printing spooler. It automatically opens (minimized on the desktop) when it has a job to do, and we can view its window to see the status of documents waiting in the queue (see fig. 16.6). It is via this window that we can halt printing in the middle if something isn't coming out as we expected.

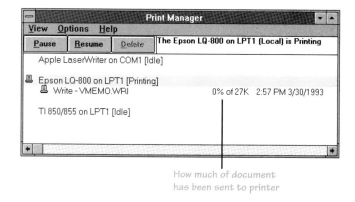

Figure 16.6
The Print Manager informs us of its progress handling spooled printing jobs.

How much of document has been sent to printer

They're Out To Get Us

Few things are as frustrating in this world as overcoming PC printing problems. So many pieces can get in the way—a weird printer, a cable, any one of several ports on the computer, the printer driver, fonts, and so on.

Another element that doesn't help the process are inconsistencies among some programs with regard to the Print Setup dialog. In fact, Microsoft is one of the worst offenders at doing out-of-the-ordinary things. For example, in Microsoft Word for Windows 2.0, the Print Setup dialog lacks the page orientation icons—page orientation has to be set in a Page Setup dialog, opened from the Format menu.

Adding a new printer to your PC may cause some initial headaches, especially if you're switching from a non-PostScript printer to a PostScript printer. Of course, you'll have to install the driver as the first task. Windows drivers for new printers usually come on a disk included with the printer. The driver may also be in the library of printer drivers supplied with Windows. In either case, they can be installed via the Printers control panel (see the 19th Encounter).

What can really throw you off is the font situation. A document created and edited with one printer selected may look entirely different when another printer is selected if very different sets of fonts accompany each printer. Again, it's best to select the printer and fonts for a document early in the game—*before* getting fancy with its formatting and appearance.

Printing problems are nightmares, because they usually occur when you're in the biggest rush to get something out. You'll pick up tips along the way from experience, such as turning on the printer before launching Windows or printing just one copy of a job to make sure that everything is all right before printing the other 24 copies.

Practice

Print Setup

1. Activate Write and open the vmemo.doc file.

2. Choose Print Setup from the Write File menu (see fig. 16.7). Notice the settings available for your printer. We'll use the default settings, as most documents do.

Figure 16.7
Choose Print Setup.

3. Click Cancel.

4. Choose Print from the File menu.

5. Click OK in the Print dialog to use the default settings.

6. Go to the printer and wait for the results.

7. Choose Print Setup from the File menu again, click the landscape button, and click OK.

Figure 16.8

Click the landscape button.

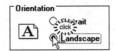

8. Choose Print from the File menu.

9. Click Print and wait for the document to print in landscape mode.

10. If you want to save this setting with the document, choose Save from the File menu.

11. Exit Write but don't save changes if you're asked.

Summary

We've learned that much of the technical wizardry of managing the printer is handled internally by Windows, with a little help from us in the Print Setup and Print dialogs. Print Setup settings are saved as part of each document. Printing subsequent copies or versions involves only the Print command and Print dialog. No matter what, a printer driver for the printer must be installed in your Windows system.

Exorcises

1. What determines the correct communications between Windows and your printer?

2. Detail the steps required to print two copies of pages 5 to 10 of a document.

3. Describe background printing and what it means to your productivity.

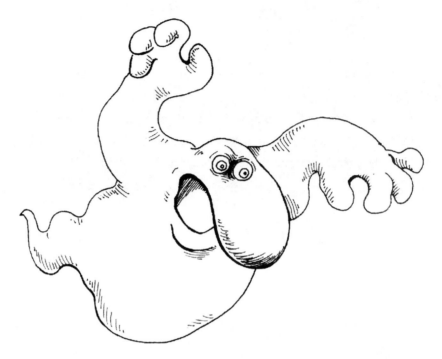

Customizing Your Desktop

Goal

Learn how to make important system settings and have Windows start up with your important applications already on the desktop.

What You Will Need

PC turned on with Windows running, today's date, and an accurate time signal.

Terms of Enfearment

control panel	Startup Group
beep sound	run minimized

Briefing

Be in Control

Buried within the Windows folder is a collection of files that give us im-
mense power over the way Windows behaves. These files are known as
control panels and are gathered together under a Program Manager icon
called, conveniently enough, Control Panel. The Windows installation
routine places the Control Panel icon inside the Main group in the Program
Manager, but if you followed instructions in the 9th Encounter, it may now
be in a group called Applications. Open that Control Panel icon, and it
produces a window showing an icon for each control panel file (extension
cpl) installed in your Windows folder (see fig. 17.1).

Figure 17.1

*Double-click the
Control Panel icon
to view icons for all
control panel files
installed in your
copy of Windows.*

Control panel icons in the Program Manager have their own pretty icons
and names to help you. To access a control panel, double-click its icon.

It's About Time

One important PC feature we can control by a control panel is the internal
clock, which keeps track of the date and time, even when the machine is
turned off. The clock is not a Windows feature: it is built into the computer
hardware (and the little Clock application in Windows continuously reads
information from the system clock). It's important to have the internal clock
set correctly, because that's where the modified dates for files come from.
You may also use programs that keep your schedule or sound alarms for
you—they *must* have access to the current date and time to be of any use.

Setting the Time

We set the clock by way of the Date & Time control panel (see fig. 17.2). It's not essential to set the clock to the second, but here's how to do it:

1. Press the Tab key a few times until the hours figure highlights and type the current hour.

2. Tab to the minutes figure and type the next minute.

3. Tab to the seconds figure and type the figure zero.

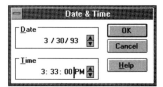

Figure 17.2
Setting the time to the start of the next minute.

4. At the sound of the tone for the next minute, press the Tab key. Depending on the speed of your PC, you may have to Tab a second or two *before* the tone.

5. With the AM or PM highlighted, press the A or P key, whichever setting is highlighted at the moment.

Setting the date is just as easy. Tab to each segment of the date and enter the appropriate values. Close the control panel when you're finished.

To close any control panel, double-click the control menu box at the top left of its window.

Mouse/Pointer Speed

I mentioned in the 4th Encounter that we can set the speed at which the pointer on the screen reacts to quick motion of the mouse. This is done in the Mouse control panel. Figure 17.3 shows the Mouse control panel that comes with Windows and supports most mice.

One element we can adjust is the Tracking Speed. The further to the right the box is along the scroll bar control, the faster the pointer moves in reaction to faster mouse motion—allowing us to cover more screen real estate with less desk real estate or ball rolling. This setting reacts instantly to the control, so you can try it out after each adjustment.

Figure 17.3
Mouse tracking adjusts how quickly the screen pointer moves in response to quick moves of the mouse.

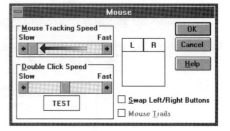

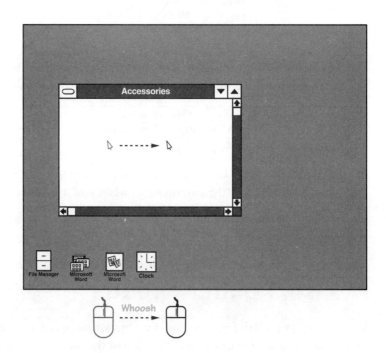

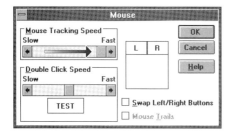

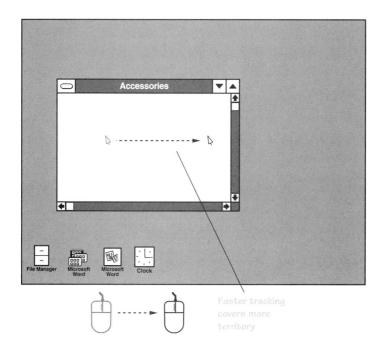

Faster tracking
covers more
territory

If your PC is equipped with a non-Microsoft-brand mouse, it may come
with its own control panel, such as the Logitech one shown in figure 17.4.
The panel offers more choices than the standard control panel.

Figure 17.4
*Substitute Mouse
control panel for a
Logitech-brand
mouse.*

Replaces Windows mouse
control panel icon

Beep Beep

In response to various actions, Windows or applications generate an audio
clue that something is wrong—like clicking outside a dialog box when the
only operations allowed at the moment are those within the dialog. Known
as the *beep sound,* the actual sound may be something quite different from a
beep *if your PC is equipped with an optional sound card* (few PCs come from
the factory equipped for anything other than a simple beep). All this is
controlled by the Sound control panel (see fig. 17.5).

If your PC isn't equipped for extra sound (or the software that came with
your board is not installed), the Sound control panel is for the most part
dimmed. The only control is a checkbox that lets you turn off even the
simple beep sound.

Figure 17.5
*Most items in the
Sound control panel
are dimmed if your
PC doesn't have
enhanced sound
capabilities.*

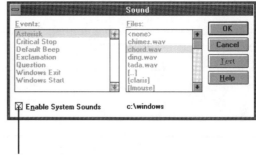

Uncheck to turn off system beeps.

For those users with sound cards, Windows comes with four sound files to play with. Use the Sound control panel to assign those sounds (or extras you acquire from more avid PC users) to specific actions that occur while using Windows, such as when certain kinds of alert dialog boxes appear (denoted by the icon that appears in the alert: Asterisk, Exclamation, or Question). Click on any sound name in the list and click the Test button to hear what it sounds like.

A sound board may even allow you to record extra sounds to add to the list. But this would be like having fun—and we're supposed to be doing our work.

And the Rest

At your leisure, you can explore the other control panels supplied by Windows. If you click on a control panel icon, a description of what it does appears in the bottom line of the Control Panel window. The Color and Desktop panels may be of interest if you want to change the color scheme and desktop pattern (see fig. 17.6). If things get out of hand, refer to table 17.1 for important default settings.

Table 17.1. Default Settings

Control Panel	Item	Default Setting
Color	Color Scheme	Windows Default
Desktop	Pattern	(None)
Desktop	Screen Saver	(None)
Desktop	Wallpaper	(None)
Desktop	Icons	75 pixel spacing

Figure 17.6
You can go nuts in the Color and Desktop control panels if you're not careful.

We'll come back to some control panels later when we learn how to extend the powers of your copy of Windows.

Automatically Starting Programs

Windows (beginning with Version 3.1) has given the Program Manager a special group, called *Startup*, that is a most helpful tool in setting Windows up for us day after day. By dragging or copying (Control-dragging) program icons to the Startup group, we instruct Windows to start those programs each time Windows itself starts up. Moreover, we can decide which program(s) should open up to their working window state and which should be open but minimized to an icon on the desktop.

For example, if one of your programs manages your daily calendar, it can start up with Windows and be ready to show you today's appointments without any further effort on your part. Without a doubt, the File Manager belongs here (see fig. 17.7) as should all other programs you tend to use frequently.

Figure 17.7
This collection means that the File Manager, Microsoft Word, and the Clock will be running each time Windows starts.

Instructing a Startup program item to open as a minimized icon requires a simple change in the Properties dialog box for that item. A checkbox, labeled *Run Minimized* should be checked (see fig. 17.8). Notice that this affects only the copy of the program item in the Startup folder—not those in other groups. Also, the order in which the icons are arranged in the Startup group window is the order in which they start—and appear on the desktop. Launching order is from left to right, top to bottom.

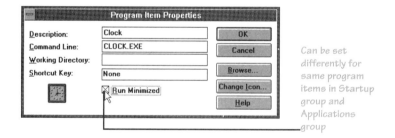

Can be set differently for same program items in Startup group and Applications group

Figure 17.8
Check the Run Minimized box in the Properties dialog of each item you want opened in minimized form.

This Startup gizmo works with documents, as well. A program item of a specific database file in that group both launches the program and loads the database during the startup process.

They're Out To Get Us

PC internal clocks remember their stuff with the help of a small battery inside the system unit. If this battery runs down, the clock won't hold its time and date—or other setup information, such as the technical characteristics of your hard disk. Unfortunately, changing one of these batteries isn't always like swapping a couple AA cells in your Walkman. It may require taking the unit in for service. These batteries should last for many years, however.

A common mistake when setting the clock is to forget adjusting the AM/PM setting. Therefore, if it is really 10:30 AM but the clock gets set to 10:30 PM, the date will rollover at your real noon, because the PC thinks it's midnight.

Practice

Setting the Date

1. Open Control Panel in the Program Manager. The Control Panel window opens, revealing all those items installed in your PC.

2. Double-click on Date & Time.

3. If the first (month) number in the date area is not highlighted, press the Tab key several times until it is.

4. Either click on the up or down arrows to cycle through the numbers or type the number of the current month.

5. Do the same for both the day and year numbers.

Setting the Time

1. Tab to the hour number and type the current hour (unless it's only a couple minutes to the next hour, in which case, you should type the next hour).

2. Tab to the minutes number and type the digits for a minute or two in the future.

3. Tab to the seconds number and type a zero.

4. If you are using a time standard (like the phone company's), call it up. Wait for the tone signaling the hour and minute in the setting and press the Tab key in synch (see fig. 17.9).

5. Click on the AM or PM designation and press the A or P key, depending on which side of noon the time will be set to.

6. Close the Time & Date window.

Figure 17.9

Setting the clock to a phone company time signal.

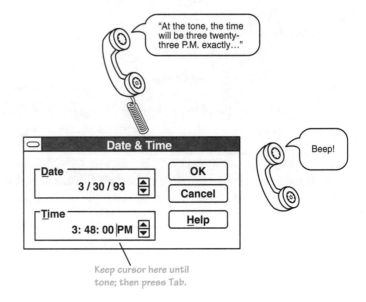

Figure 17.9

Setting the clock to a phone company time signal.

Keep cursor here until tone; then press Tab.

Setting Mouse Tracking

1. Open the Mouse control panel from the Control Panel window (see fig. 17.10).

Figure 17.10

Open the Mouse control panel.

2. Drag the Mouse Tracking scroll bar setting a little to the left and move the mouse around the desk to see how the pointer responds to your action. Adjust the scroll bar in the other direction and try the mouse again. When the mouse response feels the most comfortable, leave the scroll bar in that position.

3. Close the Mouse control panel.

Setting Beep Sound

1. Open the Sound control panel.

2. If the lists of items are dimmed, your PC either doesn't have a sound card or the driver file is not installed properly. Skip the rest of this section.

3. Click on the Default Beep item in the list of events.

4. Click on each of the sounds in the listing at the right (files with the wav extension) and click the Test button to sample each sound in the list.

5. Choose the sound that you want to hear each time Windows beeps at you.

6. Close the Sound control panel and the Control Panel window.

Summary

We have great control over Windows basic operations by adjusting control panels. If there is something about the way things look, feel, or sound, the solution may be in a control panel. We can use the Startup group in the Program Manager to instruct Windows to launch programs or documents for us each time Windows starts.

Exorcises

1. How do you access Windows control panels?

2. It's time to change all clocks to daylight savings time (turn clocks ahead one hour). Describe the steps required to keep the PC clock in synch with local time.

3. What does it mean when Windows beeps at you?

Extending Your System's Capabilities

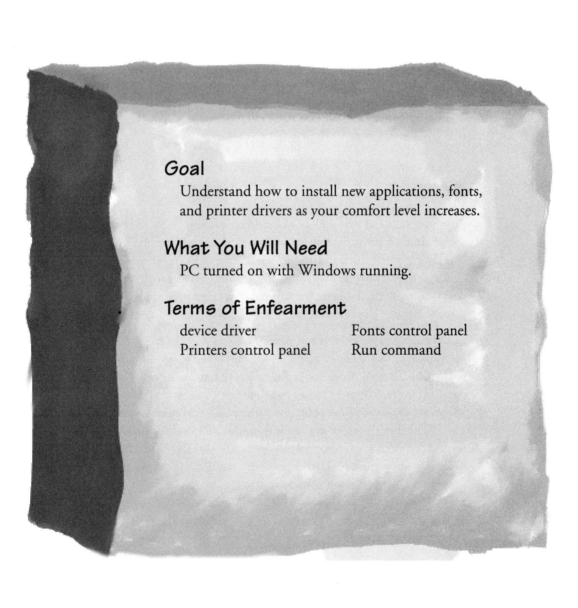

Goal
Understand how to install new applications, fonts, and printer drivers as your comfort level increases.

What You Will Need
PC turned on with Windows running.

Terms of Enfearment
device driver

Printers control panel

Fonts control panel

Run command

Briefing

A Never-Ending Story

As sophisticated as Microsoft's Windows system software is, we can actually think of its components as Lego blocks. Microsoft supplies a basic kit of parts that interlock nicely—so seamlessly that we scarcely notice the zillion files scattered around the hard disk. To software developers, however, the Windows system is something that can be modified and enhanced with the addition of more components.

Some components add to what's already there, and others replace pieces that Microsoft delivers.

Windows Own Devices

Anytime you hang a new piece of hardware off your PC and it is to be used with Windows software, you usually need to add a file called a *device driver*. A printer driver, which I introduced in the 16th Encounter, is one type of device driver. CD-ROM drives, tape backups, sound cards, optical scanners—all these need drivers for Windows to communicate properly with them.

In the case of printers (and some other devices) that existed when your copy of Windows was manufactured, drivers come with Windows. All you have to do is install them from the master disks that came in your Windows package. In the Printers control panel, for example, you can see whether Windows has a driver for your new printer. Click the Add button (see fig. 18.1). The double-arrow in that button indicates that the dialog box will expand to reveal more information. In fact, it displays a list of drivers that Windows knows about. These drivers are not yet on your hard disk—only those in the list at the top of the window are on your disk.

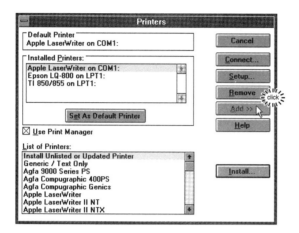

Figure 18.1
Clicking the Add button in the Printers control panel reveals a list of printer drivers that come with Windows.

Select one printer model and click the Install button. Behind the scenes, Windows figures out which disk from your master set has the driver you just selected. You'll be prompted to insert the diskette (see fig. 18.2). When you do (and click OK), Windows copies the driver to the proper place on your hard disk.

Figure 18.2
Windows asks for the diskette containing the selected driver.

Your Own Devices

The list of printers isn't the only source of drivers for Windows. After all, you may have just bought the latest whizbang printer that didn't exist when your copy of Windows came off the assembly line. But the printer (if advertised to be Windows compatible) comes with a disk containing the driver. You can access this driver from the *Printers control panel.*

The very first item in the list of printers says Install Unlisted or Updated Printer. When you select this item and click the Install button, yet another dialog comes up (see fig. 18.3), requesting the name of the driver (pre-selecting the floppy drive for you because it assumes that you'll be installing from a floppy). Use the Browse button to locate a file on the floppy disk with a drv extension—the Browse button enters error-free names into file name fields, so it's the way to go in all file name entry situations. Windows does the rest—copying the file to the System folder inside the Windows folder.

Figure 18.3

Installing a driver from a floppy disk.

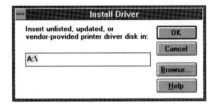

Typefaces and Fonts

As we saw in the 15th Encounter, fonts are nothing more than software elements—files in the Windows folder. Actually, font files need to be in a special place for them to load into Windows: nested in the System folder inside the Windows folder.

The *Fonts control panel* is the font manipulator for TrueType and screen fonts. As with the Printers control panel, we use the Fonts control panel to add fonts that arrive on floppy disk (or perhaps from a file server drive). We don't even have to worry about font file extensions, because as long as the disk or folder contains font files, the control panel extracts the full font family name (e.g., Times New Roman Italic) and the type of font (TrueType or screen). Select the font(s) to be installed, make sure that the Copy fonts to Windows directory checkbox is checked and click OK (see fig. 18.4).

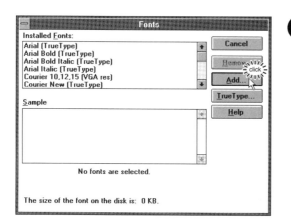

Figure 18.4
After double-clicking the Fonts control panel icon, complete these steps to add a TrueType font to Windows.

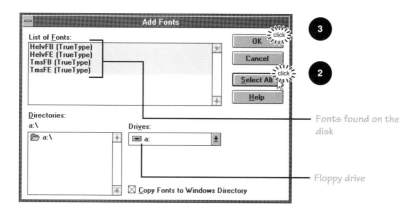

Fonts found on the disk

Floppy drive

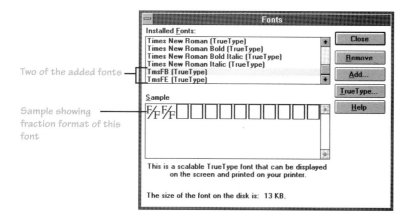

Two of the added fonts

Sample showing fraction format of this font

PostScript Fonts

Although the Fonts control panel helps us install TrueType fonts, Adobe
Type Manager, an extra utility program, is the way in for PostScript fonts.
Installation follows the same general principles as with TrueType fonts in
the Fonts control panel (see fig. 18.5).

Figure 18.5

*Use Adobe Type
Manager to install
PostScript fonts.*

Shows up as an application

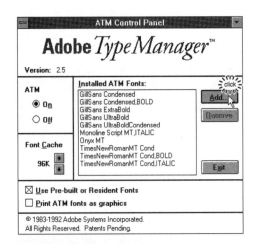

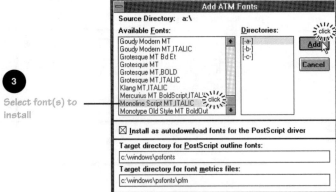

Select font(s) to
install

Installing New Windows Programs

All applications programs come with installation instructions. The most common type is the one that instructs you to issue the *Run* command in the File Manager and to type a command line that includes the setup file's name. If you're averse to typing (and who isn't?), open a File Manager window of that floppy disk (see fig. 18.6). Locate the exe file named setup or install and double-click it. That's the Windows way of doing things.

Also during program installation, you may be presented with some additional dialogs asking for input. The most common is the path for the folder that contains the program and its files. The default it provides will usually be the root (e.g., c:\nuprgm) or in the Windows folder (e.g., c:\windows\nuprgm). If you followed the File Manager guidelines in the 8th Encounter, you want none of the above. Instead, make sure that the Apps folder is in the path (e.g., c:\apps\nupgrm). Some programs will follow this instruction but also will place some stuff into the Windows folder (or in a folder nested inside the Windows folder). They say not to move what they put there—and that's good advice.

The other obnoxious thing some installers do is create a Program Manager group icon for their program and any ancillary stuff that they feel belongs in the Program Manager. If you've bought into my Program Manager organization ideas in the 9th Encounter, drag those items to the Applications group (or other group if it makes sense for your organization method) and delete the empty group icon from the program's installer.

Figure 18.6

*Starting the setup
routine of a program
installer floppy disk.*

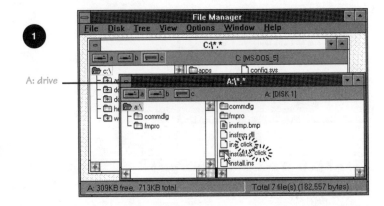

Figure 18.6

*Starting the setup
routine of a program
installer floppy disk.*

A: drive

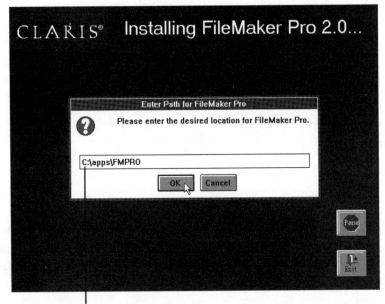

Added our apps folder to installation path

Installing New DOS Programs

Despite Windows capability to switch us out to DOS at a moment's notice,
it's best to exit Windows before installing any DOS software (unless its
installation instructions tell you differently). Because not all DOS programs

react well to Windows, the installation should take place with as clean an environment as possible. Exit Windows and proceed with installation directions provided with the program.

Some DOS programs include elements for Windows, such as icons for the Program Manager and pif files (program information files), which Windows can use to set up the DOS session for that program in the way the program's designers intended. The program's installer usually presents a screen asking whether you want to add Windows stuff to the Windows folder. Do so.

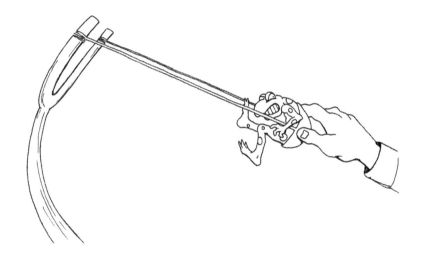

They're Out To Get Us

There is a downside to loading extra fonts and drivers into your copy of Windows. They all take up some amount of RAM when Windows starts. If you're working in a low-memory environment (anything under 8 MB of RAM), adding lots of items may cause you to see more `Out of Memory` alerts when you try to perform tasks in programs that worked before.

Program installers are a mixed blessing. They shield us from having to copy files and from knowing lots of things about our computer hardware. On the other hand, they are sometimes not intelligent enough to leave out some files that our hard disks could do without. After a dozen files have been copied into the new program's folder, it's not always easy to know which ones can be deleted to free up disk space.

When a program installer creates a Program Manager group and installs the programs item icon(s), those items won't know a thing about your hard disk organization for documents. Select the program item icon and choose Properties from the File menu. Then type c:\documnts into the Working Directory field, as I covered fully in the 9th Encounter. Failure to do this will cause Save dialog boxes to default to the program's own folder, which is some distance (in folder clicks) from the document storage part of your hard disk.

Practice

Exploring the Windows System Folder

1. In the File Manager, open the System folder that is nested inside the Windows folder (see fig. 18.7).

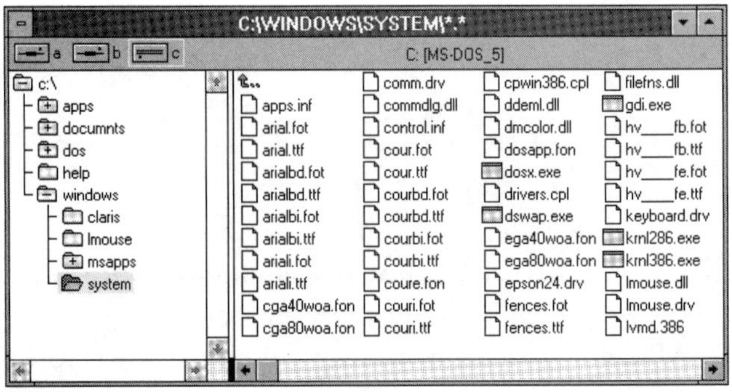

Figure 18.7

The System folder inside the Windows folder.

2. Pull down the View menu and choose Sort by Type. This sorts the list of files alphabetically by file name extension.

3. As you scroll through the files, look for groups of files with the following extensions:

cpl   Control panel
drv   Drivers (for mouse, printers, sound cards, etc.)
fon   All-purpose screen fonts (including those used for menus, icon labels, etc.)
fot   One half of a TrueType set of font files
ttf   The other half of a TrueType set of font files

These are the kinds of files that installers and control panels (such as Fonts, Printers, and Drivers) move into and out of the System folder. Windows expects these files to be in a folder named System inside the Windows folder, so don't move any of these files manually.

4. Choose Sort by Name in the View menu.

Check Out Some Control Panels

1. Open the Control Panel icon in the Program Manager.

2. Double-click the Fonts icon.

3. Scroll through the list of fonts installed in your system (see fig. 18.8). Notice that some fonts say TrueType after them, and others say things such as VGA Res or Plotter. The TrueType fonts are the ones you should use in documents going to dot matrix or non-PostScript laser printers. A separate file contains font description data for each weight (regular, italic, bold, etc.). Other fonts are meant for plotters or, more commonly, for screen display when a font specified in a document is not in the system (e.g., when someone gives you a file created on another machine).

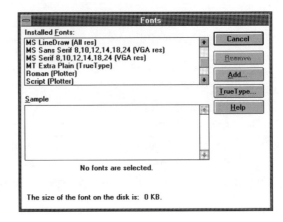

4. Close the Fonts and Control Panel.

5. Open the Write application, type a couple of words into the blank
   document, and select them.

6. Pull down the Character menu and choose Fonts.

7. Notice how in the list box in figure 18.9 the program groups together
   all variations of a TrueType font into one font listing (e.g., Arial).
   Choose the weight in the list to the right of the fonts list.

8. Close all windows and programs.

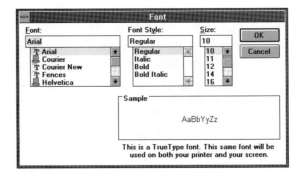

Summary

We've seen that Windows consists of a set of software pieces that we decide we need. By adding items with the help of installers and control panels, we can add functions to the basic Macintosh operation we use every day. That includes extending the selection of fonts for our text-based documents.

Exorcises

1. Someone hands you a diskette that supposedly has some TrueType fonts for your system. What steps do you follow to get those fonts into your system?

2. The label on the disk of a new Windows-based program contains the following instructions:

   ```
   * Choose Run from the Program Manager's File menu.
   ```

   ```
   * Type a:\install
   ```

   How would you install the program from the File Manager?

3. The label on the disk of a new DOS-based program contains the following instructions:

   ```
   * Type a: and press Return.
   ```

   ```
   * Type setup and press Return.
   ```

   If you are viewing the Program Manager of Windows, what steps would you follow to get this program installed?

When Things Don't Work

Goal

Learn how to track down sources of problems so that you can solve them yourself or ask the right questions.

What You Will Need

Lots of luck to never need the information in this chapter.

Terms of Enfearment

lockup	freeze
crash	#&*%@!
bug	

Briefing

On the Edge

Using a personal computer in our work can truly improve the quality and quantity of work we accomplish. But try as we might to regard the computer as just another tool, the technology can really grab us by the neck when things don't work. Moreover, we must contend with Danny Goodman's corollary to Murphy's Law:

> If something goes blooey on the computer, it happens when we have the least amount of time to deal with the problem.

The closer a deadline nears, the more likely a computer foul-up will gum up the works.

When Most Problems Occur

It's rare for a computer to go haywire by just sitting there on its own. If something breaks, it generally happens when we try to start the computer or when we issue a command for the computer or software program to do something. Because problems manifest themselves in response to our actions, it is not uncommon for us to blame ourselves, rather than the computer.

Admitting There Is a Problem

The good news is that every problem has a solution. Some solutions are easier than others, but the problems can be solved.

One of the difficulties in tracking down problems caused by Windows software installations (e.g., new programs, device drivers) is that the installers may modify files that are normally hidden from view. These files contain utter gibberish unless you're a genuine, top-of-the-Himalayas DOS and Windows guru. Adding to the potential for disaster is the unfathomable combination of PCs, their components, hard disks, video monitors and cards, mice—the list is nearly endless. The older any piece of equipment is, the more prone it is to having difficulties with Windows and its programs.

When something unexpected occurs, our most important job is to do our best to narrow down the possible sources of the difficulty. Even if the problem ultimately results in having to take the computer into the shop, the better we can define the problem, the quicker (and cheaper) the fix will likely be.

Get Terminology Right

If we plan to tell anybody about the problem, it is vital to describe the general symptom properly. Too many times, effort goes into tracking a symptom when the user misnamed the problem. Use the following handy table:

What Happens	What To Call It
All action stops, except rolling mouse pointer	lockup
Everything freezes, including pointer	crash
Error dialog box	error message
Hard disk won't mount for love or money	disk crash
Something you didn't expect	bug
Any of the above resulting in lost data	#&*%@!

Find What Works

When a problem prevents us from continuing with our work, we must begin looking for a diagnosis—at last, a chance to be the doctor our parents always wanted us to be. Assuming that the computer worked properly at some time before the problem occurred, the first task is to try to get back to the state in which things worked.

The simple fact is that a lot of problems occur when we add something new to our computer—a new hard disk, a new application, a new video card. Although the new thing may not be the real cause of the problem (the problem may be lurking, ready to leap out because of a conflict with the new item), we must reach a point at which we can safely say that adding so-and-so causes the problem.

If we have added any of the following new items, we should perform the corresponding action as a first step in diagnosis:

New Item	Action
External hard disk	Disconnect it from the PC.
Internal hard disk	Reinstall the old hard disk, if possible.
Any external device	Disconnect it from the PC.
RAM module	Restore RAM to previous configuration.
Plug-in board	Remove it.
Driver	Use the Drivers or Printers control panel to remove it.
Font	Use the Fonts control panel (or Adobe Type Manager) to remove the new font, so it won't load with other fonts upon startup.
Application	Don't start it.

This advice can be tricky at times, because an application or plug-in board software may modify one of those squirrely files I mentioned a minute ago. There may also be another Murphy's Law corollary in the wings, because it's eerily common for us to buy more than one new thing at a time and to install or connect them all in a rush. The key here, however, is to get all the new stuff out of the line of fire and make sure that we've returned to a reliable state. Then gradually add back each item one at a time and try to recreate the problem. When the problem recurs, the last item just added is the most likely suspect.

Oh, Those Files!

When things get so bollixed up that you can barely start your PC or Windows, it may be time to acknowledge the existence of four files that may contain the source of your problem. Huge volumes have been written about how to modify and tweak these files for performance improvements and incompatibility fixes, but that's not our goal here. Instead, we need to get you back up and running in Windows and then to be able to adjust those files if someone tells you what to do (e.g., when you get advice from a guru or product support person at a software company).

The four files that can contain your problem are as follows:

File	Directory	How To Pronounce It	What It Does
autoexec.bat	root	autoeggseck batch file	Loads initial programs for the system
config.sys	root	config dot siss file	Loads drivers and other configuration settings
win.ini	windows	win innee file	Loads Windows user and display preferences
system.ini	windows	system innee file	Loads Windows hardware preferences

The first two files, autoexec.bat and config.sys, are read by DOS each time your PC boots. The .ini files are read as Windows launches. All four files are simple text files, which can be viewed and edited with a text-editing program, such as Note Pad.

Probable Problems

We'll now examine the five most common symptoms of trouble and describe how best to isolate the cause for each. Unless you're faced with one of these problems, it's not important to read each in full detail. It may be helpful, however, to read through the symptoms: if one should happen to your PC, you'll know where to turn for help.

Really, Really Dead

Symptom

When you press or flip the power switch for the PC, absolutely nothing happens: no tones, no screen illumination, no disk spinning.

Nature of the Problem

Either the PC is completely fried, or the PC isn't getting power.

What To Do

1. Make sure that the PC is plugged into a live power outlet (test the outlet with another electrical item if necessary).

2. For laptop PCs, plug in the AC adapter. The battery may be fully discharged.

3. Try substituting another power cable, because a break in a cable could prevent it from carrying the requisite juice.

4. Contact your dealer about service (always the last resort).

Alive, But Barely

Symptom

The PC turns on, but instead of hearing the usual startup tone and seeing the monitor fill with DOS stuff, you see some scary-looking message.

Nature of the Problem

Your PC failed the hardware self-test it performs each time you turn on the machine. Either a component on the system board inside the computer has gone bad (very unlikely) or something isn't connected correctly.

This problem occurs predominantly after you've added something new in the hardware department: RAM modules inside the system; an add-in board; any device connected to the SCSI (scuzzy) card, such as an external disk drive or CD-ROM drive. Begin the diagnosis by removing all new items and making sure that the original setup works properly.

What To Do

1. If you've just added some new hardware or moved things around, restore the old scene to see whether the old way works. Gradually add new items back to the system until you encounter the problem.

2. Make sure that all SCSI cables (if any) are securely fastened to their connectors.

3. Make sure that all memory modules and plug-in cards are squarely seated in their sockets.

4. Make sure that all system board connectors are squarely seated in their sockets.

Disk, Please!

Symptom

The PC turns on, but instead of your hard disk spinning and DOS starting up, a message says something about a non-system disk error (see fig. 19.1).

Figure 19.1

*Non-system disk
error message.*

```
Non-system disk or disk error
Replace and strike any key when ready
```

Nature of the Problem

Your PC can't locate a disk that has MS-DOS system software on it.

What To Do

1. Make sure that all external hard disk devices are turned on and have power before turning on the PC. Remove any floppies from their drives

2. Insert a floppy disk that has a minimum system on it (as described in the 20th Encounter) and press any key. If this fails, switch off the PC and try starting again with the floppy disk. Try this once again but

disconnect any cable attached to the hard disk or SCSI card. If this last attempt doesn't make it, it's time for service, and you can skip the rest of this section.

3. If your PC doesn't have an internal hard disk, connect only the desired startup hard disk to the PC. Turn on the hard disk and wait about 30 seconds before turning on the PC.

4. For an external disk drive, try another cable, if one is available; for an internal drive, make sure that all cables between the drive and system board are securely fastened to their connectors.

5. After starting the PC with a floppy disk, use whatever backup method you prefer to make copies of irreplaceable files. The next steps may make it more difficult to recover files if the disk is damaged.

6. Obtain a disk recovery program, such as *Norton Utilities* (Symantec Corp.) or *PC Tools* (Central Point Software). Follow instructions for the product to perform a disk diagnosis. The products also will attempt to repair the damaged files.

7. If possible, try the disk drive (even if it's an internal drive) on another PC. There is the remote possibility (hey, this is the time to grasp at straws) that the system board is faulty, preventing *any* hard disk from booting.

8. With your backup files carefully saved from the hard disk, start your PC with a copy of the original MS-DOS disk (disk 1 of the set). Type FDISK at the A:\ prompt and press Enter. Unless you're told otherwise (in which case someone else should be doing this for you), follow the instructions on-screen to format your hard disk as a single partition. If the formatting fails, proceed to the next step; otherwise reinstall DOS and restore your files from the backup.

9. If you have reached this far and can't get that disk working, you're in big trouble, I'm sorry to say. The disk is so badly damaged that you'll need to send the disk to a disk recovery service. The disk drive's manufacturer may provide such a service or can direct you to a company that performs the service. Most or all of your data files are probably still intact on the disk, and some disk recovery services charge according to the number of files you ask them to save (but you have to be able to tell them which files they are).

Welcome to Win...

Symptom

The PC turns on; the hard disk spins; and you seem to be able to start Windows, but it then quits or locks up. You cannot get Windows running.

Nature of the Problem

Most commonly, a conflict exists between your PC hardware and what Windows thinks your hardware consists of. The chief problem probably lies in the system.ini file, which expects hardware other than what's on your PC.

What To Do

1. Restart your PC (Control-Alt-Delete will do) and press Control-Break after the PC's memory test finishes. If a messages asks about aborting the batch job, press the Y key.

2. Re-install Windows, letting Windows examine your configuration and setting its system.ini file accordingly.

3. If that doesn't work, the installer may be getting incorrect information about pieces of the system. If you have full specifications about your PC's innards, go through a more manual setup process by typing *setup /i* (a space between setup and the "slash-i") at the DOS prompt. Answer all questions to the best of your ability.

4. If your PC has an 80386 or 80486 microprocessor chip, try starting Windows from DOS with the following command:

   ```
   win /s
   ```

   If this works, you know that you can get Windows to operate in standard mode, even though your PC should be able to operate in the 386 enhanced mode. This is valuable information you should tell a guru or dealer. Your system.ini file may need to be modified to trick Windows into running in 386 enhanced mode.

Crashes & Faults (Not a Law Firm)

Symptom

While performing an action in Windows, the screen *freezes* or presents an error dialog box (which may say something about a general protection fault).

Nature of the Problem

Although we don't doubt there's a problem, if the problem isn't repeatable, it will be virtually impossible to diagnose or get help. It could be a program bug (unlikely), a conflict between the program and a hardware driver, or a problem between the program and some external device.

What To Do

1. If the keyboard or mouse are ineffective, suspect the keyboard cable. For a quick remedy, try unplugging the mouse and keyboard cables (without turning off the PC in this extreme case) and then reconnecting them. If you now have regained control, consider replacing the cables. If this doesn't work, try another keyboard or mouse, if you have one available.

2. For a program lockup, try pressing Control-Alt-Delete to force the current application to quit (called a local reboot). If this works, you'll regain control of the PC, but it's possible that the RAM contents have been boggled a bit. Immediately save documents in other applications, quit those applications, and restart Windows.

3. If a local reboot just completely hangs the system, it's System Crash City. Another Control-Alt-Delete should let you restart the machine. Occasional rare and spectacular crashes won't even let this warm reboot work, in which case you've got to hit the big switch (or button) that forces the machine to shut down. Laptop PCs that have a sleep mode may require the press of the semi-secret reset button on the rear panel. You then can restart the machine as usual.

4. Turn off the PC and check all cables connected to the back panel. Make sure that they're all connected securely.

5. Try to recreate the problem. If you can, the problem is probably a bug in the program. Call the software publisher about the problem. It isn't always possible for a developer to test every combination of device and driver for compatibility. Contact the program's publisher and see whether the company has other reports of the problem with your hardware setup.

Error Messages

What we've been through so far covers only the most egregious problems— some of which aren't even Windows problems per se. That leaves the dozens of error or alert messages that crop up while using Windows—Program Manager, File Manager, and other programs. Unfortunately, when these messages pop up in their windows, they often strike us as finger-pointing by the teacher: "Bad user, stupid user."

It may be difficult to overcome that sense, but we should regard these messages more as reminders that something isn't right. Consider these messages more as friendly warnings or advice.

After you feel comfortable about these messages, it may take some cool reflection to know what is really the source of difficulty. For instance, if you try to copy a folder from the hard disk to a floppy disk that happens to be locked, the sequence of messages is most bizarre: the first message requests confirmation about copying the directory to the floppy drive; the Copying progress window appears in anticipation of showing us each file as it flows from one disk to another; another window advises us that the folder doesn't exist on the destination and asks whether we want to create it; an Error Copying File dialog appears, telling us Access Denied; finally, at the bottom of that dialog comes some advice: `Make sure the disk is not full or write-protected`.

Avoiding Computing Disasters: Rules To Live By

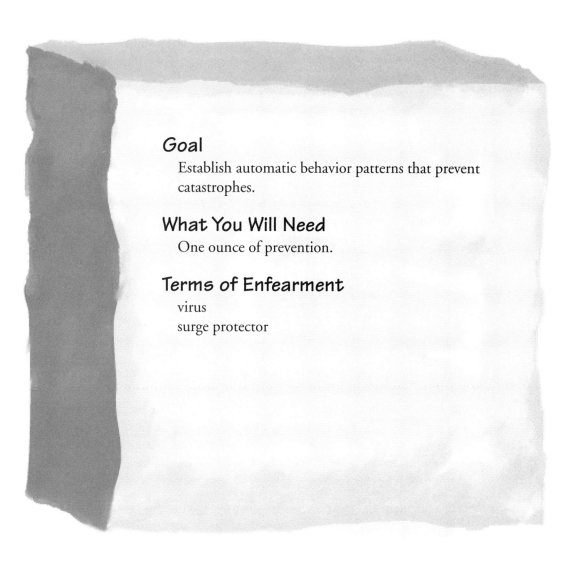

Goal

Establish automatic behavior patterns that prevent catastrophes.

What You Will Need

One ounce of prevention.

Terms of Enfearment

virus
surge protector

Briefing

If you glanced through the last encounter, your anxiety level may be up a notch or two. Some of those problems seem like genuine nightmares. Although no one or no magical device can guarantee that you won't experience some of the problems described there, you can pattern your work habits with your PC and Windows to minimize the risk of those things happening.

The following is a succinct list of little things you can do to prevent lost work or time:

1—Backup Your Data Regularly

A daily backup of your documents is the best insurance against a loss. No matter what else may befall your PC, the backup copies will enable you to restore your machine to the state of its last backup. A number of commercial backup utility programs ease the burden. With a tape drive or extra hard disk that is at least as capacious as the main one you use, the backup program could do the job while you're out to lunch or while you're getting ready to leave for the day.

2—Invest in Virus Detection Software

A *virus* is the generic term for evil little software gremlins designed by clever and sadistic computer programmers. Viruses propagate silently from machine to machine primarily through the sharing of files via floppy disks or through the transfer of files from databases over the telephone. Viruses are sometimes benign, but more often, viruses corrupt important system files, documents, and programs. If your hard disk becomes infected with a virus, the virus will be copied to any backup copy you make.

Virus detection software usually includes a background program that always runs. If it detects any of the hidden actions that viruses tend to perform, it alerts you to potential danger and can prevent the damage. Such software can also scan your hard disk(s) to see whether any known viruses are already on your disk and can remove them if so.

Importantly, virus creators try to stay one step ahead of virus detectors, so it's vital that you keep your virus detection software up-to-date. Some commercial suppliers provide a subscription service, which automatically sends out new versions of the detector when new virus information is available.

3—Keep an Emergency System Floppy Disk Handy

The bulk of hard disk problems prevent the disks from starting the PC. If you can start the PC from a floppy disk, the hard disk will more than likely be available as the C:\ drive.

Format a blank disk in the File Manager and check the Make System Disk box that copies essential files to the diskette (see fig. 20.1). If your PC and Windows are running fine at this point, drag the following files from your hard disk to this emergency diskette:

File	From
autoexec.bat	root directory
config.sys	root directory
win.ini	windows directory
system.ini	windows directory

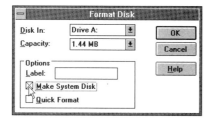

Figure 20.1
Formatting a floppy as a system disk.

This diskette is now equipped with enough system information on it to boot your PC and to start Windows. If the problem is that Windows won't run correctly, replace the win.ini and system.ini files in your hard disk with the two files from the emergency disk (which worked some time in the past). In either case, after you're in Windows, you can use the Note Pad to investigate the autoexec.bat and config.sys files on your hard disk and emergency floppy to see where they diverge—and thus perhaps find the culprit device or software that modified these files so that they don't work as expected.

4—Invest in a File Recovery Utility Program

There will be a time—guaranteed—when you will have erased a file that you desperately need again. DOS 5.0 and later comes with basic utilities to help recover files. If you haven't done a lot of disk writing since you trashed the file, the disk recovery utilities that come with DOS 5.0 or, a commercial file recovery program have an excellent chance of unerasing the file for you.

5—Lock Read-Only Floppy Disks

One reason I recommend that you lock floppy disks that won't be written on is to prevent virus infection. For example, you wouldn't want a virus to infect a master disk of an application program in case you need to re-install that program. Occasionally, a program won't let you install it from a locked floppy disk. In that case, lock and make a duplicate of the original. Install the software from an unlocked copy.

6—Turn Everything Off before Plugging or Unplugging Cables

Some users go forever swapping cables without powering down and have no problems. This is risky business, especially for SCSI cables. Worse yet, when cable switching with the power on causes a problem, it is often a case of a blown component on the PC's system board. Authorized service providers for name-brand PCs rarely replace individual board components—they replace the entire board. Under warranty, that's no big deal; out of warranty, it can be many hundreds of dollars.

7—Invest in a Surge Protector

Surges are the generic term for a number of different types of zaps from the power company. They occur for any number of reasons, all of which are out of your control: switching electrical sources in the power grid; restoring power after a blackout; a power pole being knocked down in a storm or accident; heavy electrical equipment on the same line being cycled on or off.

A *surge protector* tries to intercept the very brief, very high-voltage zaps before they reach devices plugged into them. Most economy power strips that advertise built-in surge protection aren't adequate.

8—Unplug Everything in an Electrical Storm

A direct lightning strike to a power pole feeding your place of computing will fry most surge protectors and everything plugged into them. But even a nearby hit can conduct enough juice in power lines to cause problems. Even though equipment is turned off, at least one of the lines of the AC power cord remains connected to the circuitry of your PC, providing a nice pathway for a shocker.

9—Keep at Least Five Megabytes Available on Your Hard Disk

It's easy to forget to look at the amount of free disk space. When it starts to fill up, leave some breathing room for yourself. First, you want to make sure that there's room for a new document you create and want to save. Secondly, some programs or processes, such as background printing and FAX software, write temporary files to the hard disk while they work with your documents: without the free space, the programs may not be able to complete some operations.

10—Load Your Constant Applications First

If you tend to keep one or more programs running all day, load them first thing upon startup (or put program items for them in the Startup group of the Program Manager). By occupying their memory blocks early, they will leave maximum memory available for other programs that may come and go during the day. It's also a good idea to check the Run Minimized box in these items' Properties dialog box so that they appear menu-like across the bottom of the desktop.

11—Minimize—Don't Exit

When you're finished with an application, reach for the minimize button rather than the control menu box (to exit the program). If you have sufficient RAM (real and virtual) for this practice, you lessen the likelihood that your PC's memory will get fragmented—prohibiting you from loading a program you had run earlier in the day.

12—Avoid Temperature Extremes for Laptops

With a laptop PC tucked in a briefcase, you may forget that it's been left in a hot car or lugged across a frozen city. Although the machines are built to withstand extremes when not in use, the acceptable temperature range for using things like the hard disk and liquid crystal display is much narrower. If you bring a laptop indoors after it has been sitting for awhile in extreme heat or cold, open the lid and let the machine adjust to near room temperature before starting it up.

Glossary

The terms defined in this glossary were introduced in encounters throughout the book. The icons next to each term identify the encounter in which you will find the term used in context.

(6) active window The topmost window denoted by a colored or darkened title bar.

(1) Alt key A special-purpose key used with one or more other character keys to issue commands to programs.

(11) applet Small accessory programs.

(8) (11) application Usually a full-fledged software program (as distinguished from a desk accessory).

(11) **application window** The area on the screen devoted to a single application program, featuring its own menu bar and space for working document contents. May contain one or more separate document windows.

(1) **arrow keys** Four keys used primarily to position the text insertion pointer within editable text.

(14) **associate** To link—in the File Manager—a document type (as distinguished by its file name extension) to a particular application so that opening the document also launches the application.

(19) **autoexec.bat file** A text file that contains a script of DOS commands automatically executed when the PC boots.

(16) **background printing** A process that enables the computer to send individual pages of a document to the printer while you work on other programs or documents.

(13) **backup** An extra copy of a file to be used in case the original file becomes lost or damaged.

(17) **beep sound** The sound the PC makes when the machine or a program wants the user's attention.

(15) **bitmap** A collection of pixels that form a graphic image.

(2) (10) **booting** Starting up a computer or program.

(9) **Browse button** A dialog box button that enables you to fill in a file's path field by clicking through graphical representations of folders and files instead of by typing the path.

(19) **bug** A problem, usually in application software, that causes the computer to do something other than what the program was designed to do.

(13) button On the mouse, the area you press to execute a mouse click; on the screen, an area to be metaphorically pressed by positioning the screen pointer atop that area and pressing the mouse button.

C:\> prompt See **MS-DOS prompt.**

(5) cascading menu A type of pull-down menu that displays submenus to items.

(9) cascading windows A window organization that enables some windows to partially obscure other windows, allowing many windows to be present and easily accessible.

(4) click A quick press and release of the mouse button.

(15) Clipboard A special area of memory that temporarily holds any information copied or cut.

(15) Clipboard Viewer A program that enables you to see what's in the Clipboard and to save the data to a file (or load the Clipboard from a file).

(14) close The action of removing a window from the screen.

(18) command line A prompt that waits for you to type a command.

(19) config.sys A text file that contains a script of DOS commands pertaining to drivers and other hardware controls automatically executed when the PC boots.

(1) Control key A special-purpose key used with one or more other character keys.

(14) Control-Alt-Delete The keyboard sequence that can exit a locked-up Windows program or restart the PC.

(5) control menu box The clickable area at the top left corner of windows containing commands for keyboard-only users. This area may be double-clicked to close the window (document windows) or to exit the program (application windows).

(17) control panel A software element that enables users to adjust system-level settings, such as the internal clock, desktop pattern, and other preferences.

(15) Copy The menu command used to transfer selected information to the Clipboard without harming the selected information.

(10) copying files The process of creating duplicate copies of selected files onto the same or other disk.

(19) crash A problem that causes everything on the screen to stop responding to user control.

(15) cursor keys See **arrow keys.**

(15) Cut The command that deletes selected information and places a copy in the Clipboard.

(12) database A type of program that contains any type of information divided into individual records (like filing cards).

(13) default Standard settings provided by a program without any further intervention by the user.

(2) desktop The underlying area on the Windows screen, atop which all windows lie.

(18) device A hardware item that connects to the basic circuit board of the PC, either directly or through an adapter card. A device also may be software that emulates an external device, such as a RAM-based electronic hard disk.

device driver See **driver.**

dialog box A screen window that provides information to the user or requests the user to enter information.

dimmed item A menu appearing in gray that does not respond to selection by the mouse.

directory A grouping of files and other directories, represented in the File Manager as a folder. Directories inside other directories may also be called subdirectories.

directory tree The File Manager diagram of directory folders.

directory window A File Manager window that displays the tree and contents of a single directory. The name of the window changes as other directories are opened.

diskette See **floppy disk**.

diskette drive A mechanism that reads information from and writes to a floppy disk.

document An information container created by an application.

document window The screen area—inside an application window—where you view or edit a document. Some programs allow for multiple document windows. In no instance does a document window overlap and extend beyond the boundary of its application window.

double-click A rapid series of two clicks of the mouse button.

double-sided One type of a floppy disk, capable of storing approximately 720 kilobytes of information.

drag-and-drop The process of dragging one icon to another and releasing the mouse button.

dragging Clicking and holding the mouse button down while sliding a selected item across the screen.

15 draw object A graphic element, such as a circle, that can be manipulated as a single entity, rather than a series of pixels (**bitmap**).

7 drive A representation of a storage device, identified in DOS and in the File Manager by a letter. Drives A and B are usually floppy disks, but hard disks, file servers, and other devices begin with the letter C.

18 driver A file that contains instructions allowing the PC to communicate with a device.

5 drop-down menu Choices available by clicking and holding down an entry in the menu bar.

5 Edit menu A pull-down menu found in many Windows programs that allows cutting, copying, and pasting of information.

13 eject The process of removing a floppy disk from a 3 1/2-inch diskette drive.

1 Enter key The key resembling the typewriter's carriage return key, which sends commands typed at prompts or into dialog boxes.

1 Escape key A special-purpose key that is often the equivalent of clicking an on-screen Cancel button.

14 exit The process of stopping a program and removing it from memory.

7 extension The last three letters of a file name, following a period.

13 field A screen space for entering text information, much like a blank in a form.

8 file An element stored on a disk, usually a program or document.

3 **7** File Manager A Windows system software program that enables you to organize, to erase, and to locate disk files.

(5) **File menu** A pull-down menu in virtually all Windows programs that contains commands for file-oriented tasks, such as opening, saving, and printing.

(7) **file name** In DOS (and therefore Windows), an identifying title by which each file is known in the directory. A file may consist of eight characters plus a period and a three-letter extension. Also spelled as one word, filename.

(6) (13) **file server** A disk that appears as a volume in one PC's File Manager, although the physical disk may be located in another computer, connected via a network.

(13) **fixed disk** See **hard disk.**

(7) **floppy disk** A soft magnetic material (similar to cassette tape) housed in a plastic shell used for storing computer files.

(15) **floppy drive** See **diskette drive.**

(7) **folder** A screen representation of a container for one or more files and folders; also called a **directory.**

(15) **font** A collection of letters, numbers, or other characters following the same typographic design.

(13) **format** The process of preparing a storage medium to accept information for later retrieval.

(1) **Function keys** A series of special-purpose keys on the standard PC keyboard.

(12) **graphics program** Any application that lets the user create graphical information.

(3) **group** In the Program Manager, a collection of one or more icons representing programs or document files.

(3) **group icon** A small representation of the group window. All group icons are alike but may be named differently.

(3) group window The window that appears when a group is opened. The window contains program item icons.

(3) hard disk A mechanical device capable of storing large amounts of computer data, resembling the functionality of a large filing cabinet. Hard disk contents are remembered after the computer is turned off.

(5) Help menu The rightmost pull-down menu of the menu bar that offers access to a program's help system.

(13) high-density One type of a floppy disk, capable of storing approximately 1.2 to 1.4 megabytes of information.

(2) icon A screen representation of an electronic item (for example, file, folder, disk, menu command).

(6) inactive window A window not currently in the frontmost position.

insertion point See **text insertion pointer.**

(5) keyboard equivalent The keyboard sequence (often including the Alt key) that performs the same action from the keyboard as choosing a menu item.

(7) kilobyte A measure of information capacity, roughly equivalent to 1,024 typed characters.

(16) landscape printing The Print Setup dialog specification that lays out printed information so that the paper is wider than tall.

(10) launch Start a program.

(13) list box An area in a dialog box that contains a scrolling list of choices that can be easily selected by a click or double-click of the mouse button.

(13) locked disk A floppy disk whose write notch is covered (5 1/4-inch diskette) or whose locking tab is set (3 1/2-inch diskette), preventing information from being written to the disk.

(6) maximize An upward pointing arrow button in the upper right corner of a window that instructs the window to occupy the entire screen. When the window is full-screen, the button changes to a **restore** button.

(7) megabyte A measure of information capacity, roughly equivalent to 1,024,000 typed characters.

(7) memory A place for temporarily storing information while working with it (see also **hard disk**). Memory contents disappear when the computer is turned off.

(3) menu bar The screen element stretching across the top of a window, containing pull-down menus used to issue commands to the computer or a program.

(6) minimize A downward pointing arrow button in the upper right corner of a window that instructs the window to shrink to an icon. When the window is minimized to an icon, a double-click of that icon restores the window to its previous size.

(4) mouse A palm-sized device (with one or more buttons) tethered to the computer, which is used to control the location of the screen pointer and to invoke action (by pressing a button).

(4) mouse button The pressable switch on the mouse.

(2) MS-DOS Microsoft Disk Operating System, the software that enables personal computer users to manage disks, files, and other aspects of the hardware via commands typed at the MS-DOS prompt.

(2) MS-DOS prompt The characters on a screen (usually ending with a >) advising the user that the computer is ready to accept an MS-DOS command. Sometimes referred to by the drive letter, such as the C:\> prompt (pronounced "see-prompt").

1 numeric keypad A grouping of keys containing only numbers and arithmetic symbols to simplify entering numbers (also sometimes a separate smaller keyboard device).

15 Open dialog A dialog box used to navigate through disks and folders to locate a file for opening within a program.

11 palette A small window usually containing icons for a program's tools or graphics choices.

15 Paste An Edit menu command that places (when possible) the contents of the Clipboard into the active document window.

7 path The text line that contains the sequence of directories, usually starting with the drive letter, leading to a file. Also called the *pathname.*

11 **18** PIF Program Information File, a Windows file that contains instructions for Windows to manage RAM, video, and other aspects of a non-Windows program launched from within Windows.

3 pointer The icon that moves on the screen in response to the rolling motion of the mouse.

13 pop-up menu A menu style, usually found in dialog boxes or document windows, that enables the user to view, on request, a list of choices.

16 portrait printing The Print Setup specification that lays out printed information so that the paper is taller than wide.

16 PostScript A printing technology by Adobe Systems that defines characters by mathematical descriptions of their outlines, rather than by an arrangement of pixels. Preferred over TrueType by professional typesetting service bureaus.

16 Print dialog The dialog box seen after choosing Print from the File menu, allowing the user to choose the number of copies, page range within a document, and other printer-specific settings.

16 Print Manager The Windows spooling program.

16 Print Setup A File menu command that leads to a dialog box allowing choices of printed page orientation and other printer-specific settings.

16 printer driver A file that contains conversions allowing the computer to speak the language of a given printer.

16 **18** printer font A file that contains outline specifications for a printer to use in producing characters.

11 program Any application that turns the computer into a tool for working with information or managing the computer.

program information file See **PIF**.

3 program item An element in a Program Manager group window, represented by an icon, that refers to a program or document that may reside anywhere on the hard disk.

3 Program Manager The Windows program that provides simplified access to frequently used programs.

9 properties The attributes of a file or icon representing a file.

7 RAM Random Access Memory, the memory area used by programs and documents.

14 restart The process of turning on the PC again without completely shutting down the machine via the Control-Alt-Delete keyboard command.

6 restore A double-arrow button at the top right corner of a window that returns a window to the size and location prior to maximizing; also, the action of returning a window to its previous size from a minimized desktop icon.

1 Return key Key that behaves similarly to the carriage return key on a typewriter.

7 root directory The most basic level of a volume, which you see when opening a disk in the File Manager.

17 **run minimized** The process of starting an application that displays itself only as a minimized icon on the desktop.

13 **Save** The File menu command that writes a copy of a previously saved, open document to disk.

13 **Save As** The File menu command used to give a name to a new document or to save a copy of an existing document.

13 **Save As dialog** The dialog box used to assign a name to a document and to direct the location where the file is to be saved.

18 **screen font** A file containing specifications for displaying a font in a particular size on the screen.

6 **scroll bar** A window control element that shifts the document vertically or horizontally to view other parts of a document.

10 **Search** The File Manager command that locates all files meeting specified name criteria.

4 **selecting** Clicking an item or dragging across text to signify what is to be affected by the next command.

13 **SneakerNet** An informal way of referring to transferring information between computers via floppy disk.

16 **spooling** The process of letting the computer perform communication with an external device (e.g., a printer) as a background task, while the user works in other programs or documents.

12 **spreadsheet** A type of application that replicates on screen the ledger sheet of columns and rows of numbers.

17 **Startup group** A special group in the Program Manager whose contents are automatically started each time Windows starts up.

subdirectory See **directory**.

20 **surge protector** A device inserted between your computer and the power outlet that prevents sudden high-voltage surges from reaching and possibly damaging the computer.

(19) system.ini An initialization file that Windows uses to accommodate various hardware devices inside or connected to your PC.

(15) text cursor A style of screen pointer used to establish the position of the text insertion pointer.

(12) text editor A program that allows typing and editing of text characters.

(15) text insertion pointer A flashing vertical line between characters that indicates where the next typed character will be inserted.

(9) tiled windows A window organization that places windows side-by-side, so that no window overlaps any part of another window.

(6) title bar The window element stretching across the top of the window that displays the window's title and is used for dragging the entire window around the screen.

(11) toolbar A thin series of graphical screen buttons that usually act as shortcuts to common menu commands.

tree See **directory tree.**

(6) (18) TrueType A printing and screen display technology that defines characters by mathematical descriptions of their outlines, rather than by an arrangement of pixels.

(15) Undo The Edit menu command that takes back, when possible, the last command that altered a document.

(11) utility A type of program usually devoted to system software adjustments or maintenance.

(20) virus A dangerous, usually hidden program written by sociopaths that can cause erratic behavior with your PC, including damaging the hard disk. Its effects can be thwarted by virus-detection programs.

(7) virtual memory A system function that enables a portion of a hard disk to act as additional RAM.

6 volume A storage device or file server whose icon appears on the desktop.

10 wildcard A character in an MS-DOS file name that can be any character for the purposes of finding matches. The question mark stands in for a single character; the asterisk stands in for any number of characters up to the limits of DOS file names.

19 win.ini An initialization file that Windows reads upon startup to set a number of visual and other operating parameters.

3 window A movable and resizable rectangular space on the screen in which any program-related action takes place in Microsoft Windows. See also **application window** and **document window**.

6 window border The draggable straight edge of any window for resizing horizontally or vertically.

window control menu See **control menu box.**

6 window corner The draggable corner of any window for resizing in any direction.

9 working directory The path applications use as the default for Save As dialog boxes.

Epilog

What To Do When You Don't Know What To Do

My goal with this book was to equip you with basic Windows skills so that you could begin using the computer as a productive part of your daily work life. I avoided all the minutiae that DOS and Windows power users relish. If you should ever develop a genuine interest in computing as an end unto itself (instead of computing as a means to accomplishing your job), there are plenty of books, magazines, and user groups to satisfy every curiosity.

If you're like most readers, you will soon develop patterns for the way you use Windows that you won't even think about. You'll tend to start up the same program(s) day after day. You'll cut, copy, and paste the same way day after day, whether choosing the commands in the Edit menu or adopting the keyboard equivalents. When using your computer daily, you will develop habits similar to those developed by drivers—like instinctively reaching for the headlight switch in your car as it gets dark. When you get to your destination, you may not even remember exactly when you turned on the lights.

Although knowing basic skills is critical to being productive with Windows, the true measure of proficiency is how well you handle unexpected situations. I have been preparing you for that all along.

What Kind of Unexpected Situations?

The 19th Encounter showed you how to confront any of those lockups, crashes, or bugs that get in your way. Every problem has a solution. Do your best to remain calm and follow the suggestions for each problem listed there.

Another situation likely will involve figuring out how to perform a procedure you're not familiar with—or uncovering whether the desired action is possible with the software you're using (including the Program Manager and File Managers). Master the following sequence, and you'll always find what you need:

1. Pull down each menu.

2. Try each menu command ending with an ellipsis (...) to find clues to dialog boxes.

3. Consult the Help menu.

4. Look for help in the product's manual under every relevant term you can think of.

5. Get help from real people at product support or your corporate help desk.

Fear No More

Despite the apparent complexity of personal computers, especially if you are a newcomer, it is easy to be an intelligent user. No one should expect you to know it all. It's far more important to know where to begin looking for help—somewhere between the menu bar and technical support—than to worry about having all the answers on the tip of your tongue.

If you began this book with fears about using Windows, I sincerely hope that practicing basic skills in the preceding encounters have shown you how easy Windows computing can be. Overcoming fear of the unknown takes just a little practice—most of which you've already had. Now it's time to put your newly acquired skills to work, doing what you do best.

Relax and flourish.

Answers to Exorcises

1st Encounter

1. 12

2. c

3. Hold down the Alt and Shift keys and then press the F5 function key.

2nd Encounter

1. booting

2. MS-DOS

3. command prompt or DOS prompt

3rd Encounter

1. win.com

2. desktop; the Desktop

3. windows

4. Clockwise from top: b, e, c, a, d

4th Encounter

1. select

2. pressing the mouse button; rolling the mouse; releasing the mouse button

3. double-click the icon

5th Encounter

1. The menu selection leads to the display of a dialog box.

2. select something

3. double-click the control menu button

4. Windows makes sure that all documents are saved and closed properly.

6th Encounter

1. Clockwise from upper right corner: d, g, f, c, b, h, a, e.

2. a. Allows us to resize the corner of the window; b. Scrolls the contents of the window down one line or unit; c. Scrolls the contents of the window down one window-full; d. Allows us to move the window around the screen; e. Shrinks the window down to an icon.

7th Encounter

1. 25 working days

2. Clockwise from top: a, c, b, d.

3. File Manager icons are generic, but Program Manager icons are larger and usually contain icon art derived from the application.

8th Encounter

1. directory or subdirectory

2. directory tree

3. The folder is selected, yet nothing appears in the right pane: the folder is empty.

4. You must bring the destination folder into view (without selecting it) before dragging the file to it.

5. The document will go into the Apps folder, because it's the one that is highlighted.

9th Encounter

1. group icon; program item icon

2. Properties

3. The working directory is the path a program presents as the default for saving documents; the command line is what you would type from the root DOS prompt to start the program.

10th Encounter

1. Using the File Manager, select in the directory the folder containing the file you wish to copy, scroll the tree so that you can see the destination folder, and drag the file icon to the destination folder icon.

2. Select each folder that contains files you can remove from the hard disk. Use the View menu to sort the lists by the method that helps you locate removable files (e.g., sort by date to find the oldest files at the bottom of the list). Select all removable files. If those documents can be deleted, choose Delete from the File menu or copy them to a floppy disk as an archive of important files and then delete the copies on the hard disk.

3. Look through all your document folders and change the list view to sort by date. Optionally, use commands in the View menu to display the last modified date details in the file lists. Select and drag the found files to another drive.

11th Encounter

1. Open the group icon containing the program's icon; double-click the program's icon.

2. There is no precise number, because each application occupies a different amount of RAM, and virtual memory can allow many more applications to be open without adding RAM.

3. If the other program is visible behind the current program, click on its window; otherwise, hold down the Alt key and press the Tab key until the desired program's name appears in the small window on the screen.

4. a. Look for the name of the program in the active window's title bar; b. Pull down the Help menu and see the program's name in the About menu item.

5. Go to the Program Manager and add a new program item inside a group; Browse your way to the pif file in the 123 folder and double-click it, entering the proper command line into the Properties dialog; then close the Properties dialog for the 1-2-3 icon.

12th Encounter

1. The program usually has an application window in which multiple document windows may be located. A maximized document window places a second restore button inside the document window.

2. The total usually depends on the amount of memory assigned to the program and in your PC.

3. Clockwise from upper right corner: a, c, d, e, b.

4. On the smaller control menu button at the upper left

5. The application and document shrink to one desktop icon labeled for both the program and document.

6. Try in the following order: a. Type a few characters to see whether they reach the window; b. Look for a New command in the File menu; c. Look for a tools palette and select a tool to use with the pointer; d. Look for menus that lead to dialog boxes; e. Access the on-line help via the Help menu; f. Read the manual.

13th Encounter

1. File menu

2. Save assumes the document already has a name and location in a folder, so it doesn't query you for naming the document; Save As leads to a dialog box requesting a file name and folder location.

3. True

4. The command triggers the Save As command.

5. Each time you reach a point at which you don't want to re-do work because the power went out or the computer hangs.

6. Absolutely. A floppy disk is like any volume.

7. Either click the drive icon or choose Refresh from the Window menu.

8. Select the file in the list view and choose Delete from the File menu. To erase a diskette, choose Format Disk from the Disk menu and fill in the appropriate fields to format the disk in the floppy drive.

14th Encounter

1. Close, Exit, or Quit; the commands are always available in the control menu and sometimes in the File menu.

2. Yes: saves the current state of the document before closing the window; No: discards all changes and closes the document or program; Cancel: takes back the close command, leaving you at the same spot you were before issuing the command.

15th Encounter

1. a. Cut or Copy a selected item or chunk of text; b. Use the Clipboard Viewer accessory to open a file previously saved via the Viewer.

2. Paste

3. Select the old text and start typing the new.

4. Open the Clipboard Viewer accessory and save the information to a file (which you must open via the Viewer in the next session).

5. a. Select the paragraph with a click at the beginning and a Shift-click at the end; b. Choose Cut from the File menu; c. Position the text insertion pointer at the desired location; d. Choose Paste from the File menu.

16th Encounter

1. The printer driver selected in the Print Setup dialog.

2. a. Choose Print from the File menu; b. Tab to the range fields and type 5 and 10 into the fields; c. Click the OK button.

3. Background printing sends information to the printer chunk by chunk as the printer is able to accept data, while you can go about doing other tasks. You can be working in a different program while a long document prints out.

17th Encounter

1. Double-click the Control Panel icon in the Program Manager. The resulting window displays icons for each control panel installed. Then double-click the panel of your choice.

2. a. Open the Date/Time control panel; b. Press the Tab key three times until the hours digits highlight; c. Type the number for one hour ahead of the time displayed there; d. Click the OK button.

3. The computer or a program that's running wants your attention, either because you tried to do something that isn't allowed at that moment or because your input is required to complete a task.

18th Encounter

1. Insert the disk into the floppy drive; open the Fonts control panel; click the Add button; select the floppy drive; select the fonts showing in the resulting list; click the OK button; close the Fonts control panel.

2. Insert the disk into the floppy drive; click on the drive icon; locate the file named install.exe and double-click it.

3. Insert the disk into the floppy drive; choose Run from the Program Manager's File menu; click the Browse button; navigate to the floppy disk directory; double-click the file named setup.exe; click the OK button in the Run dialog.

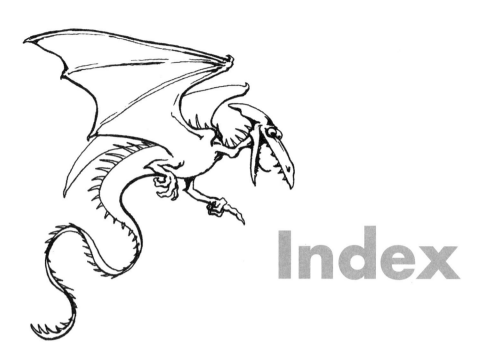

Index